AMPHIBIANS

AMPHIBIANS

by Billy Roche

WARNER CHAPPELL PLAYS

LONDON

A Time Warner Company

BILLY ROCHE

Billy Roche was born in Wexford, Eire in 1949. Starting out as a singer, he appeared as a supporting act at the Wexford Festival and went on to form his own group, The Roche Band, who released two records in the 1970's. In 1980, Billy began his writing career and his first novel *Tumbling Down* was published in 1986. His first stage play, *A Handful of Stars*, was staged at the Bush Theatre, London in 1988 and won the John Whiting Award and Plays and Players Award for Best Play. His next play, *Poor Beast in the Rain*, won the 1989 George Devine Award and the Thames Television Award. As writer in residence at the Bush Theatre, he wrote *Belfry*, the final play in the *Wexford Trilogy*, which won the London Fringe Award for Best Play of 1991. *Amphibians* is Billy's first commission from the Royal Shakespeare Company, where the play premiered in 1992. Billy lives in Wexford with his wife Patti and their three daughters.

First published in 1992
by Warner Chappell Plays Ltd
129 Park Street, London W1Y 3FA

Copyright ©1992 by Billy Roche

ISBN 0 85676 161 3

This play is protected by Copyright. According to Copyright Law, no public performance or reading of a protected play or part of that play may be given without prior authorization from Warner Chappell Plays Ltd, as agent for the Copyright Owners.

From time to time it is necessary to restrict or even withdraw the rights of certain plays. **It is therefore essential to check with us before making a commitment to produce a play.**

NO PERFORMANCE MAY BE GIVEN WITHOUT A LICENCE

AMATEUR PRODUCTIONS
Royalties are due at least fourteen days prior to the first performance. Licences will be issued upon receipt of remittances accompanied by the following details:

Name of Licensee
Play Title
Place of Performance
Dates and Number of Performances
Audience Capacity
Ticket Prices

PROFESSIONAL PRODUCTIONS
All enquiries regarding professional rights (other than first class rights) in the United Kingdom and Eire should be addressed to Warner Chappell Plays Ltd, 129 Park Street, London W1Y 3FA.

Enquiries for all rights other than those stated above should be addressed to Curtis Brown Group Ltd, 162-168 Regent Street, London, W1R 5TB.

CONDITIONS OF SALE
This book is sold subject to the condition that it shall not by way of trade or otherwise be re-sold, hired out, circulated or distributed without prior consent of the Publisher. **Reproduction of the text either in whole or part and by any means is strictly forbidden.**

Printed by Commercial Colour Press, London E7

For Gerry

AMPHIBIANS was first performed by the Royal Shakespeare Company at The Pit Theatre, London, on 26 August, 1992, with the following cast:

BROADERS	Sean Murray
HUMPY O'BRIEN	Lalor Roddy
ZAK	Barry Lynch
VERONICA	Jane Gurnett
ISAAC	Kevin Burke
SONIA	Lesley McGuire
EAGLE	Ian McElhinney
DRIBBLER	Albie Woodington
BRIDIE	Hilary Cromie
MOSEY	Liam O'Callaghan
BRIAN TAYLOR	Richard Bonneville

Directed by Michael Attenborough
Designed by Michael Taylor
Lighting designed by Geraint Pughe
Music by Richard Brown
Songs by Billy Roche

CAST

(in order of appearance)

BROADERS - *A young man in his twenties*
HUMPY O'BRIEN - *A wizened young man in his twenties*
ZAK - *A dark, handsome young man*
VERONICA - *Mid-to-late thirties*
ISAAC - *Her son, thirteen years old*
SONIA - *EAGLE'S sister, a beautiful, dark young woman*
EAGLE - *Married to VERONICA, a rugged, handsome man*
DRIBBLER - *Mid-to-late thirties*
BRIDIE - *A sad-dyed woman in her thirties*
MOSEY - *BROADERS' grandfather, a rugged old man*
BRIAN TAYLOR - *A good looking young man in his late twenties*

The play is set in the present in Wexford, a small town in Ireland.

SETTING

For the First Act the stage is divided into three sections. The main stage setting is the space that leads up to The Menapia Seafood Factory. The gates of the factory are situated against the back wall. Nets and ropes and barrels and rusty old lobster pots, etc, are strewn in the weeds that flourish all around. Outside the gates, which is the main acting area, heaps of mussel sacks are piled in various groups on the ground or stacked on the hand trolley that is used to take them into the factory. A water barrel stands close by and a glowing brazier. A crumbling wall looks down onto the sea and behind the gates we can see an old dilapidated boat which is cluttered with Wellington boots, wooden crates and a rusty tar can, etc.

The second section is the kitchen, perhaps mounted on a raised dais, surrounded by mussel sacks and bleeding into the set. It consists of a table and chairs, a sink, a fridge, a dresser, etc.

Downstage right, a little overgrown graveyard nestles beneath a gnarled old tree.

For the Second Act, the factory gates and the mussel sacks, etc, are cleared to become Useless Island, a deserted but strangely enchanted island that lies a few miles from the shore. A hut is built with wooden pilings that are lashed together with rope and sheets of plywood are nailed to the sides, and the whole lot is covered with tarpaulin.

The little graveyard remains throughout. In the Second Act there is also a scene set in the back room of a public house - a few tables and chairs and a piano, etc.

ACT ONE

Darkness. BRIDIE'S *voice sings.*

> I let my hair down
> I slipped my shoes off,
> Danced like an angel
> But I still didn't win his heart.
>
> Leaves of a willow
> Under my pillow,
> Calling him softly
> As I slumbered . . .

The lights rise. Early morning. We are outside the factory gates. BROADERS *is kneeling beside a glowing brazier, heating up the blade of his knife.* ZAK *and* HUMPY *are close by.*

BROADERS   Yes, it's reddenin' up nicely Humpy.

HUMPY   What's that?

BROADERS   I say it won't be long more now boy!

(*Slight pause.*)

HUMPY   What are yeh lookin' at Zak?

ZAK   Your man divin' off the shelter wall there.

HUMPY   Oh yeah. Did yeh see that Broaders? The new fella in the office is divin' off the shelter wall. He has all the gear on him, look - flippers and frogsuit and all boy. He's divin' down around there this past few days, yeh know . . . Cute enough too, ain't he? You'd never know what yeh'd find down there boy.

ZAK   Go away, there'd be nothin' worth talkin' about down there.

HUMPY	I don't know Zak! Yeh never know! But sure he pulled a rake of stuff out of there the other day.
BROADERS	Someone should tell that fella to leave things where they fall.
HUMPY	He's queer and spooky lookin' from here though Zak, ain't he? Whist, the Lonesome Boatman is on the horizon lads.
ZAK	Hah?
HUMPY	Eagle . . . on his way home there. Do yeh see him? With a boat full of nothin' hah! He was out for about seventeen hours or somethin' the other day there Broaders, I heard, and do yeh know what he caught? Two things - A load of fresh air and his death of cold! (*He laughs.*)
ZAK	Well at least he's a tryer, yeh have to give him that.
BROADERS	Yes! (*The blade.*)
HUMPY	Do yeh hear that Broaders? Eagle's a tryer according to Zak.
BROADERS	Start rollin' up your sleeve there Humpy.
HUMPY	What?
BROADERS	You heard me.
HUMPY	Ah no Broaders, that's not fair now. That looks redder to me than it was for any of the rest of yez.
BROADERS	Look, just roll up your sleeve there and stop actin' the baby all the time.

HUMPY	Yeah well I don't see why I should have it hotter than it was for anybody else.
BROADERS	It's no hotter than it ever was.
HUMPY	It is, Broaders!
BROADERS	Zak, is that any hotter than it was for you or me?
ZAK	No, it's the very same.
HUMPY	It's not Zak.
BROADERS	Come on will yeh, before it goes cold on me.
HUMPY	This better not hurt me Broaders.
BROADERS	Hold his arm steady there Zak. The mark of the crab, hah! Come on.
	(BROADERS *brings the red hot blade down on* HUMPY'S *arm.* HUMPY *cries out in pain. Lights down. Lights rise on the kitchen where* VERONICA *is busy preparing the breakfast.*)
VERONICA	(*calling off*) Isaac, come on will yeh, your breakfast is ready.
ISAAC	(*off*) What?
VERONICA	Come on, I'm puttin' your breakfast on the table now.
ISAAC	(*off*) Right.
	(VERONICA *takes up the porridge and lays it on the table, etc.*)
ISAAC	(*entering*) Any sign of me Da yet?
VERONICA	No.

ISAAC	He's late ain't he? He must be gone out to the island to finish off me hut or somethin'.
VERONICA	Sit down will yeh.
ISAAC	Yeah, right . . . Is this mine here yeah?
VERONICA	Yeah.
ISAAC	Are you goin' down town today, Ma?
VERONICA	Probably, why?
ISAAC	Would yeh be able to get me a diary?
VERONICA	What are yeh wantin' a diary for?
ISAAC	I'm wantin' to write down everything that happens to me tommorow night like yeh know - goin' out to the island and all. Will you be able to get me one though?
VERONICA	I don't know. We'll see. (*A sound overhead.*)
ISAAC	That sounds like one of me pigeons back already.
VERONICA	Stay where yeh are, you. Your pigeons will be alright.

(ISAAC *whistles out to the pigeon.* SONIA *enters.*)

SONIA	How are yeh Veronica? Is Eagle here?
VERONICA	No. He went out fishin' last night Sonia and he's not back yet. Why, what are yeh wantin' him for?
SONIA	Ah it's just that today's the last day if he's wantin' to put his name down for that auld job that's goin' in the factory. Will he be long more, would yeh say?

VERONICA	I don't know to tell yeh the truth. He's never this late.
ISAAC	I'm tellin' yeh Ma he's gone out to finish off me hut. He's takin' me out to the island tomorrow night yeh know, Sonia.
SONIA	Yeah I know.
ISAAC	Anyway there's no way is me Da goin' to go to work in that auld factory Ma and you know that. No way boy!
SONIA	Shut up you and eat your breakfast . . . What will I do Veronica? Will I stick his name down anyway? I will. Sure what harm, if he takes it he takes it.
ISAAC	I'm tellin' yeh Sonia, he won't work there.
SONIA	Ain't that awful Veronica. (*She pretends to choke him.*)
ISAAC	How did yeh get on with your man after?
SONIA	Mind your own business you.
VERONICA	Oh, that's right, you had a date with young Taylor last night didn't yeh. How did yeh get on?
SONIA	Alright.
VERONICA	Where did you go?
SONIA	He took me down to the Railway Hotel. We had a meal there.
VERONICA	Is he nice?
SONIA	Yeah, he's alright. A bit grand I suppose, but . . . I'll tell yeh all about it tomorrow. The walls have ears here like, yeh know.

VERONICA   I know.

ISAAC   You should have heard what me Da said about him.

SONIA   What?

ISAAC   He said he wouldn't be runnin' that factory at all only he inherited it off his grandda.

SONIA   He'd hang yeh wouldn't he?

ISAAC   Yeh should have seen him though, Ma. All the jewellery on him boy! Great big rings on him and all. I'm not coddin' yeh he was like King Faruk gettin out of the car.

SONIA   (*laughs*) He was too. But sure it's good to see someone in the family goin' out with a bit of class ain't it?

VERONICA   Are yeh goin' to see him again?

SONIA   I don't know. I might. If I'm asked of course.

VERONICA   So poor Zak is gone out of the picture altogether now then, yeah?

SONIA   Long ago. Where have you been girl? He turned up stocious drunk to see me one night and he had Broaders and that other latchico Humpy O'Brien hangin' out of him. I ran 'em. And that was that as far as I was concerned.

VERONICA   Yeah?

SONIA   Yeah . . . Well yeh can't let them walk on yeh can yeh? You're too soft with Eagle, Veronica. Yeh should put your foot down with him. How long more is he goin' to hold out anyway? I mean he's not catchin' anythin' worth talkin' about lately as far as I can see.

VERONICA	Yeah, well, yeh know Eagle . . . To tell yeh the truth Sonia, I don't like to think of him workin' in that auld factory anyway. He'd go mad - clockin' in and out of there everyday and answerin' to someone all the time.
SONIA	It's a pity about 'im. I mean to say he's out there now struttin' around the place and actin' the big fella while you're here worrying yourself sick about where the next meal's coming from. I know what I'd do with him, I'd hop off 'im. I mean has he any idea how bad things are round here?
VERONICA	I don't know. Probably not. When Eagle's out on that water you may forget about 'im. It's all up here - over his head.
SONIA	But sure you're worse, Veronica to put up with it.

(VERONICA *sighs*.)

VERONICA	No . . . He loves that auld boat though yeh know. He's in his element out there so he is. And he works hard.
SONIA	I know he works hard Veronica. No one's sayin' he don't work hard. But it's not bringin' home the bacon though, is it? I mean he could be bringin' home over two hundred pounds a week out of that factory yeh know and that's nothin' to be sneezed at.
VERONICA	Yeah I know but . . . I just don't want him to be unhappy or anythin' yeh know.
SONIA	But sure that's ridiculous Veronica. I mean to say we're all unhappy . . . Well I'm goin' to stick his name down anyway. Listen I've to go. I'll drop in to see him this evenin' some time. You'll be after talkin' a bit of sense into him by then won't yeh?

ACT ONE

VERONICA Me? You must be jokin'. He's your brother, you can talk to him.

(SONIA *leaves*. VERONICA *sighs*.)

ISAAC You're worse Ma. Sure you know as well as I do that me Da won't take a job there. No way boy!

VERONICA Yeah well let's just hope he caught somethin' decent last night then.

ISAAC Why?

VERONICA Oh no reason . . . Are you wantin' another sup of tea in that?

ISAAC Yeah.

VERONICA Yes, please!

ISAAC Yes, please. Whist, there's another one of me pigeons back I'd say.

VERONICA Finish your breakfast will yeh.

(ISAAC *whistles out to the pigeon.* EAGLE *enters, a salmon in each hand. He stands in the doorway, wiping his feet in the mat. He holds the fish aloft and winks at the boy.*)

ISAAC Oon the Da boy! There's a couple of me pigeons back already Da.

EAGLE (*laying the fish down in a box by the door*) So I see.

ISAAC They got back before yeh Da, hah?

EAGLE Yeah.

ISAAC Where did yeh let them off?

EAGLE Useless Island.

ISAAC	Not too bad for their first time out though Da is it? They'll come home all the time now, won't they?
EAGLE	Oh yeah.
VERONICA	Sonia was here lookin' for yeh. Did yeh see her?
EAGLE	I saw her goin' down the bank there. I wasn't talkin' to her or anythin'. What did she want?
VERONICA	She said today's the last day if you're wantin' to put your name down for that job that's goin' in the factory.
	(EAGLE *thinks about it and shrugs.*)
EAGLE	What do yeh think?
VERONICA	It's up to you.
EAGLE	Of the fish I mean.
	(VERONICA *sighs and turns away.*)
ISAAC	(*crossing to examine the fish*) Don't mind them Da. The pair of them are only tryin' to sell yeh down the river here boy.
VERONICA	Isaac, you get back to the table and finish your breakfast and stop actin' the auld man there all the time.
ISAAC	I'm finished. These are two right ones alright Da, ain't they? They should fetch a few bob alright, shouldn't they? Hah?
EAGLE	(*at the sink*) Yeah.
ISAAC	Will I bring them over to the factory for yeh Da before I go to school?

EAGLE	If yeh like.
ISAAC	Auld Mosey'll get some land when he sees these won't he? He was sayin' only the other day that there's hardly anythin' worth catchin' out there any more.
EAGLE	Yeh have to know where to look for them yeh see.
ISAAC	Oon the Da boy!
EAGLE	I actually caught four of them only I had to throw two of them back. Yeh should have seen them Veronica. There was all these scabs and sores all over them and their eyes bulgin' out of their heads. I've never seen anythin' like it. Of course it's all the dirt they're pumpin' into the river all the way down. Bloody scandalous so it is!
ISAAC	Did yeh do any more work on me hut?
EAGLE	Yeah, it's nearly finished now. I've just to throw the auld roof on her this evenin' and then it'll be done.
ISAAC	So we're on schedule then?
EAGLE	Yeah. Tomorrow night's the night boy! Hail, rain or snow.
ISAAC	Does the hut look alright though?
EAGLE	Yeah, it looks grand to me anyway.
ISAAC	Is it big?
EAGLE	Big enough.
ISAAC	And is it the same as the one you had when you were a young fella?

EAGLE	(*taking off his boots*) More or less. The only difference is you have a bed raised up off the ground. I had to sleep on the floor - a rake of stones stickin' into me back all night long. Yeh might get us me slippers up under me bed there Isaac will yeh?
ISAAC	What? Yeah right. I can't wait to see it boy. The smell of your feet Da!

(ISAAC *leaves. Pause.*)

VERONICA	You're not serious about this are yeh?
EAGLE	How do yeh mean?
VERONICA	You're wantin' to bring a thirteen year old boy out to a pitch black island in the middle of the winter and leave him there alone for the night. Are yeh mad or what?
EAGLE	But sure it's only a stone's throw away woman. I mean what's goin' to happen to him anyway? Nothin's goin' to happen to him.
VERONICA	He could fall into the fire. He could fall into the water. His hut could go up in a blaze or some queer fella might happen on him. I mean to say anythin' could happen to him. And he's not well either. His chest is still at him.
EAGLE	Go away, it'll harden him up a bit.
VERONICA	He's hard enough.
EAGLE	He's too soft Veronica. He needs to harden up a bit or they'll all walk on him.
VERONICA	Too soft me eye. Did you know that he was fightin' again out on the street yesterday. I had to go out after him. Too soft is right. Jaysus yeh won't be happy until yeh have him as bad as yourself - pigeons and dogs and boats! Well I'm goin' to tell yeh one thing,

Mister but if anythin' happens to that young fella out on that island tomorrow night you may pack your bags and get out of here because I'll swing for yeh. Yes, yeh may pack your bags boy.

(*She goes outside to fetch milk.* ISAAC *returns.*)

ISAAC   There's two more of me pigeons back now Da.

EAGLE   Did yeh put them in?

ISAAC   Yeah I went out on the roof and put 'em in.

EAGLE   Good. Hey, what's all of this I hear about you fightin' out on the street yesterday, eh?

ISAAC   Who told yeh that?

EAGLE   Your Mammy's just after tellin me there. What were you fightin' for?

ISAAC   I don't know. He said somethin' about me Aunty Sonia.

EAGLE   What did he say about her?

ISAAC   I don't know. I don't remember.

EAGLE   Did yeh win?

ISAAC   It was a draw.

EAGLE   Yeh lost then.

ISAAC   I didn't lose Da. It was a draw I said.

EAGLE   Isaac, how many times do I have to tell yeh, there's no such thing as a draw in a fight son. Yeh either win or yeh lose. Now which was it?

ISAAC   I won of course. Only for me Ma came out and stopped me I would have killed him.

(EAGLE *chuckles.* VERONICA *returns.*)

VERONICA Isaac, were you out on that roof?

ISAAC Yeah, I went out to put me pigeons in.

VERONICA Well I hope yeh closed that window after yeh, did yeh? I don't want them cats gettin' in again.

ISAAC (*putting on his jacket*) Yeah, I closed it. I'll bring the fish over to the factory for yeh now, Da.

EAGLE Yeah right. That's not a bad auld catch though Veronica is it? Hah? There's about forty five quid's worth there, yeh know.

VERONICA Yeah and if the Bailiffs catch yeh fishin' for salmon at this time of the year you'll end up losin' your boat and all over them.

EAGLE Make sure yeh get a docket for them Isaac won't yeh? And tell auld Mosey I'll be over to collect the money meself later on as soon as I get a bit of sleep.

ISAAC Alright.

VERONICA You don't stay too long over there Isaac or you'll be late for school, do yeh hear me?

ISAAC Yeah. But sure he never says anythin' to me now anyway. I'm the teacher's pet since you joined the school committee. Did yeh know that Da?

EAGLE What?

ISAAC Mister Collins the teacher is mad about me Ma.

EAGLE What?

VERONICA	Don't mind him. Go ahead. And listen, be careful goin' down that auld bank.
EAGLE	Yeah, mind my fish.
	(ISAAC *leaves*. VERONICA *throws* EAGLE *a dirty look. Lights down. Lights rise. It is early morning. We are outside the factory gates.* BRIDIE *is having a quick smoke inside the gates.* ZAK *and* BROADERS *are sitting on top of a stack of mussel sacks.* HUMPY *is steeping his arm in the water barrel.* DRIBBLER *enters.*)
DRIBBLER	Whenever you fellas are ready now. What's supposed to be wrong with him, eh? (*Referring to* HUMPY.)
ZAK	I don't know, Dribbler. A big crab is after bitin' him on the arm I think.
HUMPY	Very funny Zak.
DRIBBLER	Give us that auld song now Bridie.
BRIDIE	You'll be lucky . . . What ails him? (HUMPY.)
BROADERS	Who, Zak? He's broken hearted Bridie. Sonia is after givin' him the big heave-ho sure. Did yeh know that Dribbler?
DRIBBLER	What?
BROADERS	Sonia.
DRIBBLER	What about her?
BROADERS	She's after givin' Zak the shove in order to go out with a little nancy boy in an office.
DRIBBLER	Ah now, yeh don't tell me.
BROADERS	Oh yes, Mister New Boss man if yeh don't mind.

Dribbler	Aye?
Broaders	What do yeh think of that Bridie?
Bridie	But sure a change is as good as a rest Dribbler, ain't it?
Dribbler	Now yeh said it Bridie.
Broaders	Well that was always your motto anyway Bridie wasn't it. Hah? (*He sings.*) . . . I let my hair down. I slipped my drawers off. Danced like an angel but I still didn't win his heart . . .
Bridie	I think I'd be wastin' me time droppin' me drawers in front of you somehow or other.

(Humpy *laughs.*)

Broaders	I don't know Bridie!
Bridie	He's like a jackdaw when he laughs ain't he! (Humpy.) Stick a feather up his hole now and he'd nearly fly away.

(Bridie *exits. The boys laugh.*)

Broaders	What do yeh think of that Zak? Sonia walkin' to work be Jaysus! You'd think your man'd give her a lift in the mornin's at least wouldn't yeh? Hah?
Zak	Will you go and cop on to yourself Broaders.

(Broaders *laughs.* Mosey *enters.*)

Mosey	I hope you fellas are comfortable there now are yez?
Broaders	Yeah.
Mosey	Where are these out of now? (*The mussel sacks.*)

DRIBBLER	Just behind the shelter there.
MOSEY	And is that the last of them?
DRIBBLER	No, I'd say we'll get another load out of her.
MOSEY	Right. Well I suppose yeh'd better start gettin' them in to them.
DRIBBLER	Right lads, come on. Start shiftin' them.
BROADERS	Here you two, come on. Meself and Dribbler'll take in the next one.

(HUMPY *goes around to the back of the trolley and starts pushing.* ZAK *goes to the front.*)

MOSEY	What's there anyway? Three dozen?
DRIBBLER	Forty bags.
BROADERS	Look at him, he's a weak. (HUMPY.)
DRIBBLER	Bring back some empty sacks and yeh comin' Zak, will ye?
BROADERS	Yeah, and yeh needn't bother stayin' in there half the day either, tryin' to chat up Sonia!
MOSEY	He'd better not.
BROADERS	Zak is ragin'. What are yeh blushin' for Zak?

(ZAK *gives* BROADERS *the 'V' sign.* BROADERS *chuckles.* ZAK *and* HUMPY *exit.*)

Strange auld world we're livin' in too though lads, ain't it? Hah? Your man there wants a girl that he can't have and this fella here is after a woman that nobody else wants. I don't know.

DRIBBLER	What can yeh do with a fella like that Mosey, eh?

MOSEY   Don't ask me.

DRIBBLER   Well you should know Mosey, he's your grandson.

MOSEY   True he's my daughter's boy alright but to tell yeh the truth I don't recognise him out of her. Sometimes I think his poor Ma must have threw away the baby by mistake and reared the shit instead.

(DRIBBLER *sniggers.* BRIAN *emerges over the crumbling wall with a wooden chest. He is wearing a frogsuit, etc.*)

BRIAN   Hey Dribbler, give us a hand here will yeh.

DRIBBLER   What? Yeah right . . . Lord Jaysus ain't that awful. No rest for the wicked boy! What have yeh got there Boss? Treasure Island be Jaysus? Them that dies be the lucky ones hah!

(DRIBBLER *carries the chest and lays it down.*)

MOSEY   Where did yeh find that Boss?

BRIAN   Just below the shelter wall there. Open her up there Dribbler.

DRIBBLER   Yeah right. Put your hand to that Mosey, will yeh. That's it. It's not too bad inside either lads, look.

MOSEY   Oh that's a well made little casket boy.

BRIAN   It is ain't it?

(*The chest is full of ropes and maps and books and other mouldy stuff.*)

DRIBBLER   (*plucking a telescope from the chest*) Wait 'til I see what me Ma is up to.

MOSEY	Look at that. (*He finds a ship in a bottle.*)
DRIBBLER	(*looking through the telescope*) Jaysus for a minute there I thought sure the circus was in town. It's only Bridgey Malloy's big drawers on the line.
BRIAN	This auld chest used to belong to me grandfather one time Mosey. Look, there's his name there. Edward Taylor. You'd never know what you'd find in this would yeh?
MOSEY	No.
DRIBBLER	You'd want to be careful Boss. Yeh could find an auld will in there disinheritin' yeh or somethin'.
BRIAN	What? He must have threw it out the window in a fit of rage one day or somethin' Mosey hah?
MOSEY	That'd be him alright!
DRIBBLER	I can't see a thing through that . . .
BRIAN	(*peering into a dirty glass canister*) Yeh know Mosey, I was just thinkin' there that if we cleared out the bed of the shelter it could be an ideal place for plantin' mussels wouldn't it?
MOSEY	But sure that's where most of the boys moor their little boats all the time.
BRIAN	I'm sure we could accommodate them somewhere else Mosey. I mean to say that'd be ideal for us wouldn't it?
MOSEY	It'd be handy alright.
BRIAN	We'll see Mosey, hah . . . There seems to be some sort of an auld notebook in here Mosey

	. . . Give us a hand with this yoke Dribbler, will yeh? (*The chest.*)
DRIBBLER	Yeah. Anythin' for a chocolate biscuit.
	(DRIBBLER *and* BRIAN *exit with the chest.*)
BROADERS	He's only in the place a wet day be Jaysus and already he's tryin' to tell us where to moor our boats. He'll be lucky!
MOSEY	What's the matter with you? Did somebody do somethin' on yeh or what?
BROADERS	What? (*He backs away from* MOSEY'S *honest eyes.*)
ISAAC	(*entering with the salmon*) Here y'are Mosey, me Da sent these over to yeh.
BROADERS	Bardógs be Jaysus?
ISAAC	You shut up Broaders. They're bigger than anythin' you ever caught anyway.
BROADERS	Yes, a couple of sardines.
ISAAC	What do yeh think of them Mosey? Right ones ain't they? Yeh have to know where to look for them yeh see Mosey . . . He said that you're to give me a docket and he'll be over to collect the money himself later on - as soon as he gets a bit of sleep.
MOSEY	Right.
ISAAC	Me Da was sayin' that these should be worth about forty five quid yeh know.
MOSEY	Could be.
BROADERS	He'll be able to buy yeh a decent bike now so.
ISAAC	I have a bike Broaders.

BROADERS	Yeah, an auld crock of a yoke. Yeh can hear the rattle of it a mile and a half away.
ISAAC	But sure you've n'er a bike at all.
BROADERS	I tell yeh I'd sooner walk than to have to ride that thing that you have because the whole place do be laughin' at yeh. How much did he pay for it anyway - nothin'?
ISAAC	If he did then it's twice more than you paid for yours.

(ZAK *and* HUMPY *enter.*)

ZAK	(*laughing*) Hey Broaders, Humpy is after gettin' the greatest slap in the gob he ever got.
BROADERS	What? Why?
ZAK	One of the boys inside put his hand up Bridie's skirt and she blamed Humpy. Look at the big red mark on his face.
HUMPY	No though, Zak, someone inside there is after makin' allegations about me and I'm goin' to tell yeh one thing but if I find out who the alligator is they'll be gettin' a solicitor's letter in the post next week so they will.

(DRIBBLER *enters.*)

BROADERS	Hey Dribbler, this fella is after molestin' your beloved in there yeh know.
DRIBBLER	What?
BROADERS	He put his hand up her skirt.
DRIBBLER	Hey boy.

HUMPY	You shut up Broaders. Don't mind him Dribbler.
ZAK	She gave him the greatest slap in the gob that he ever got Dribbler, I'm not coddin' yeh.

(*They laugh.*)

DRIBBLER	I'm goin' to tell yeh one thing Mosey but your man is over the moon about all the things he's after findin' over the past few days here yeh know. I mean to say that auld chest is full of treasure and he has a cardboard box in there too that full of stuff - books and files and photographs and ledgers and all the rest of it - a load of stuff belongin' to his auld grandda in it there is.
MOSEY	Aye?
DRIBBLER	Yeah. Well I'm after gettin' a right cowboy book out of it anyway. "Duel In The Sun", by Chris Mortimer. You'll see me now about twelve o'clock tonight and I'll be walkin' bandy and everythin' after readin' this . . . Oon Isaac me boy! The size of the fish!
ISAAC	Me Da caught these last night Dribbler. What do yeh think of them?
DRIBBLER	Show, give us a look at them.
ISAAC	Right ones Dribbler, ain't they? Yeh have to know where to look for them yeh see.
BROADERS	A couple of bardóg, be Jaysus.
HUMPY	Yeah, sardines on toast.
DRIBBLER	One of them'd remind yeh of Humpy, wouldn't it? That fella there. The face of it.
HUMPY	Oh stop Dribbler will yeh, you're killin' me. A real Max Bygraves goin' around yeh are.

DRIBBLER	Humpy was in a picture one time when he was a young fella you know. It was called "The Reason Why Father Left Home" - He played the reason.
ISAAC	Did yeh know that me Da is takin me out to the island tomorrow night Dribbler?
DRIBBLER	Yeah I know, he told me. Did he finish off your hut yet?
ISAAC	Not yet. He's goin out to put the roof on it tonight he said and that'll be that then. He's after buildin' me a sort of a bed in it too, I think - raised up off the ground. That's no harm Mosey, is it?
MOSEY	Harm? No. Why?
ISAAC	No reason.
DRIBBLER	Jaysus they were the days though Mosey weren't they? Hah. Twelve years of age boy and yeh'd be sent out to spend the night alone on that auld island. You'd come back in the mornin' and you'd be afraid of nothin' or no one again. There's three fellas there and they're afraid of their lives to walk home alone in the dark at night after a dance.
HUMPY	Me Da was tellin' me somethin' about that alright Dribbler. They used to set the hut on fire in the mornin' didn't they?
DRIBBLER	I'll never forget the mornin' I was comin' back. I could feel the heat of the fire on the small of me back as I was gettin' into the boat and I could hear the auld crackle of the hut and that, yeh know. I was dyin' to turn around and look back at it, boy I'm not coddin' yeh. Yeh weren't supposed to look back at it yeh see. And as we were nearin' the shore I could see all the people comin' out of their houses

and down the auld bank to the beach - women
and children and auld men and everythin' and
they all wavin' and callin' out to me and all.
Jaysus it was a really magic feelin' alright
though. Auld Bridgey Malloy used to always
bake a cake for whatever boy was goin' out.
And poor auld Matty O'Brien - your Da,
Humpy, God be good to him - got the scours
after atin' it. They had to fumigate the island
after him. The rest of us used to just throw
her cake away into the water when we got out
there. I'd swear that's what ruined the
harbour in the end, Mosey.

ISAAC   Why did they stop goin' out there Dribbler?

DRIBBLER   Ah I don't know. It just sort of died out over the years really. But sure your Da was the last boy to go out to the island yeh know.

(ISAAC *smiles.*)

BROADERS   I don't think I'd fancy spendin' a night alone out on an auld haunted island though lads would you? Hah?

ISAAC   Will you go away Broaders, it's not haunted.

BROADERS   It is. The Dempsey Twins - every Saturday night!

ISAAC   Ha ha Broaders, I'm goin' out on a Friday night.

BROADERS   Or Friday night I meant to say though.

ISAAC   Yeah sure Broaders.

HUMPY   But sure there's an auld wild boar out there too this weather yeh know. I was out there last week and I saw all this wild boar shit all over the place out there.

BROADERS	Oh that's right, I was readin' somethin' about that in the papers alright.
ISAAC	There's no such thing as wild boars in this country any more, Broaders.
BROADERS	Yeah, and then yeh woke up.
ZAK	Leave him alone Broaders, will yeh.
BROADERS	What?
ZAK	Leave the chap alone out of that.
BROADERS	Is there somethin' wrong with you or somethin' Zak? Hah?

(*Slight pause.*)

ZAK	I'd say it was a good auld crack though Dribbler was it?
DRIBBLER	Yeah, it was a good auld crack alright. Every boy'd come back with his own story to tell like yeh know.
ZAK	Mmn . . .
BROADERS	I think yez are all gone soft in the head or somethin'. Buildin' huts and settin' fire to them! That all died out years ago! There's what yeh want now. The mark of the crab burnt into your arm!
HUMPY	Yes!
BROADERS	Show them yours, Zak. Come on out of that will yeh?

(BROADERS *forces* ZAK *to roll up his sleeve. He holds both their arms aloft.* HUMPY *joins them.*)

Blood brothers, boy!

DRIBBLER	There y'are now Mosey, that's what I've got to put up with all day.
MOSEY	Come on Isaac, let's go. And we'll let these fellas get back to work.
	(MOSEY *and* ISAAC *exit.*)
DRIBBLER	Poor auld Eagle, hah! Yeh have to hand it to him boy, he won't lie down.
BROADERS	What's it all in aid of though, Dribbler, that's what I'd like to know. What's it all in aid of . . . ? Bardógs!
HUMPY	Sardines on toast!
DRIBBLER	Come on, before Mosey rears up on us all.
	(DRIBBLER *wheels around and gives* HUMPY *a playful slap in the face.*)
HUMPY	Hey Dribbler cut it out will yeh.
DRIBBLER	You keep your hands to yourself in future boy.
ZAK	You'd want to be careful Dribbler or you'll be gettin' a solicitor's letter in the post next week.
HUMPY	Very funny Zak. Give us a verse of 'You Need Hands' now while you're at it.
	(*The men laugh and go about their work. Lights down. Lights rise. It is mid-morning.* BRIAN *is out at the gate checking the clocking-in cards.* MOSEY *is sitting close by smoking his pipe. Across the way, behind the factory gates, we can see* BROADERS, ZAK, DRIBBLER *and* HUMPY *working, lugging the wet mussel sacks and loading them onto the*

trolley, etc. BRIAN *takes a diary from his coat pocket.*)

BRIAN Hey Mosey - That was an auld diary belonging to my grandfather in that auld jar.

MOSEY Aye?

BRIAN Yeah. I was readin' the first few pages of it. It seems he was delighted with himself when he discovered this place here. 'An abundance of seafood', says he, 'lies untapped just below the surface. I do believe I've found what I've been looking for.' I'm hopin' it'll trace his rise to prominence in the area. But sure maybe I'll learn somethin' out of it Mosey, hah! Maybe it'll teach me how to handle all the boys if nothin' else. Because to tell yeh the truth there are times when I can't make head nor tail of them all. I mean to say one minute they're all over yeh and the next they'll turn around and nearly ate yeh. I don't know.

MOSEY They've a strange way of showin' their affection alright haven't they?

BRIAN They surely have. What did they all make of my grandda when he first arrived here Mosey?

MOSEY They didn't like him. He was too much of a what-do-you-call-it - a dictator. But sure most of them refused to work for him at first. Mind you things were a little better around here then than they are now. Your grandda didn't give a toss about any of them of course. He wasn't after their fish anyway. He wanted the crabs and the eels and the cockles and the mussels and all the other little auld slippery things that the rest of us thought we were kind of above catching. It was all out there to be taken - for nothin'. And boy was he the fella to take it too. It wasn't long until he prospered out of it. He built himself a mansion, drove around the place in a big Mercedes. Women and children is all he had workin' for him at first but soon some of the boys started bringin' him odds and ends - a bucket full of this, a box full of that. There was none of them mad about doin' it of course but most of them had no choice in the matter because they weren't catchin' anythin' worth talkin' about. He let it all go to rack and ruin then in the end be Jaysus!

BRIAN Someone told me that you never sold him anything, Mosey.

MOSEY No.

BRIAN How come?

MOSEY Ah I don't know . . .

BRIAN He'd be surprised to hear that you were workin' for me now if he was still alive wouldn't he? Hah?

MOSEY (*chuckling*) . . . Ah sure we're queer auld hawks up around here like, yeh know . . . Did yeh ever hear the story about the two fellas who built the boat together? Just to illustrate to yeh now the kind of mentality that you're dealin' with. These two fellas built a boat together right, and it was their pride and joy. Machusla they called it and every mornin' they could be seen sailin' out over the bar and across the harbour, the best of friends. But unfortunately they could agree on nothin'. All day long the pair of them fought like dogs, arguin' about everything under the sun - football and women and drink and what have yeh. In the end they winded up boxin' on the auld shingly beach below and the partnership was dissolved there and then. 'What about the boat?' says one of them. 'We'll saw it in half', says the other fella. 'You can take your half and I'll take mine and that'll be that.'

But the first fella really loved the boat and he
just couldn't bring himself to saw it in half.
So he told the other lad he could keep it.
'Well there's no point in you comin' back to
me in six months time now and tellin' me that
you're wantin' it back or anythin',' says your
man to him. 'Because I'd just as soon saw it
in half now and be done with it.' 'No,' says
the first fella, 'the boat's yours.' So the fella
that had just inherited the boat went off and
he inveigled his brother-in-law into the firm
with him and the two of them got on like a
house on fire, never a cross word between
them by all accounts. So much so that after a
few weeks of this the fella who owned the
boat got so browned off that he bet his
brother-in-law out of it one day with a big
stick and he went up to his auld mate's house
to beg him to come back and work with him
again. Well now the story goes that these two
fellas were together for a good while after and
that you could hear them debatin' across the
harbour every mornin' if you listened close.
Machusla creakin' beneath them.

(*Pause.*)

BRIAN That's a good story, Mosey.

MOSEY Yeah but it's not the way it really happened
though - in real life I mean. I know because I
was one of the men who owned the boat and I
did actually saw it in half.

BRIAN Yeah? And what about the fella who loved it?

MOSEY (*rising*) Son, I was the fella who loved it.

(MOSEY *heads towards the others.*)

BRIAN Nice one Mosey . . . Hey, yeh might tell
Broaders I'm wantin' a word with him while
you're in there, will yeh.

MOSEY	Yeah, right.
	(SONIA *arrives*.)
BRIAN	Sonia!
SONIA	I'm wantin' to put me brother's name down for that auld job that's goin' here.
BRIAN	Who? Eagle? But I didn't think he wanted to work here.
SONIA	He's changed his mind.
BRIAN	Alright. Anything else?
SONIA	How do yeh mean?
BRIAN	Well I just thought while you're here yeh might want to ask me out again or somethin', that's all.
SONIA	What? Who do you think yeh are eh, God's gift or somethin' . . . Jesus!
BRIAN	What? . . .
SONIA	Look, what happened between you and me last night as far as I'm concerned was . . . (*Words fail her*.)
BRIAN	I'm only jokin' yeh . . . Are yeh wantin' to come out for a drink with me tonight or what?
SONIA	I don't know. I might.
BRIAN	Yeah well as soon as yeh make up your mind about it yeh might give us a shout will yeh.
	(*Pause.* SONIA *looks into his eyes.* BRIAN *smiles.* SONIA *chuckles.*)
BRIAN	Will I pick yeh up at the house?

SONIA	Ok.
BRIAN	About half seven?
SONIA	Twenty to eight. Pick me up at Eagle's place though will yeh. I'm wantin' to see him about somethin'.
BRIAN	Right.

(BROADERS *arrives*.)

BROADERS	Are you wantin' me?
BRIAN	Yeah, just a minute . . . I'll see yeh tonight then Sonia.
SONIA	Yeah, right.

(*She looks into* BROADERS' *angry eyes and leaves*.)

BRIAN	It's about your time keepin' Broaders.
BROADERS	What about it?
BRIAN	I see you were late two mornin's again this week.
BROADERS	I wasn't late this mornin'.
BRIAN	No yeh weren't this mornin', but you were late yesterday mornin' and the mornin' before that too. And I see yeh never came back after dinner last Thursday at all.
BROADERS	Look if you've a complaint about my work just say so will yeh and be done with it.
BRIAN	I've no complaints about your work.
BROADERS	No I wouldn't think so either. Because I do more than my fair share. I lift twice as much as any of them in a day - more than Dribbler or Zak or any of them.

BRIAN	Yeah, when you're here yeh do.
BROADERS	Well I don't know what you're worryin' about last Thursday afternoon for anyway because there was nothin' to be done here. I saved yeh half a day's wages.
BRIAN	I would've found yeh somethin' to do, don't you worry about that.
BROADERS	Like what?
BRIAN	Cleanin' up the place inside, sweepin' the factory floor, whatever.
BROADERS	I'm employed to work the trawler not to sweep floors.
BRIAN	Look Broaders, if you don't like the way I'm runnin' things around here then there's plenty of other fellas that'll gladly take your place.

(BROADERS *scoffs*.)

	What?
BROADERS	Do you know how long I've been fishin' that harbour and sailin' that water? Since I was that high. I used to go out with me Grandda Mosey all the time. I had me own boat when I was thirteen years of age. And now just because I turn up late for work a few mornin's you're wantin' to . . . I was here long before you arrived Mister, and I'll be here long after you're gone, too.
BRIAN	Spare me the lecture will yeh and just get here on time in future.
BROADERS	Is that all?
BRIAN	Yeah.
BROADERS	Right.

ACT ONE

>(BROADERS *storms off*. BRIAN *watches him go and then he goes back into the office*. ZAK, HUMPY, BROADERS *and* DRIBBLER *are working out in front of the gates now*.)

ZAK What did he say to yeh Broaders?

BROADERS He's wantin' to give me a rise.

HUMPY Yeah, up the arse, out the door.

BROADERS Humpy, how would you like to find yourself standin' on your head in that auld water barrel for the next twenty minutes eh?

>(*A siren is blowing. All the men go to their coats for their sandwiches and flasks, etc. Some of the workers have come out of the factory to sit in the open air*. BRIDIE *comes across to join* DRIBBLER. SONIA *is sitting on the wall, away from the others*. ZAK *goes to her*.)

HUMPY Look at the size of that big crab Broaders - crawlin' out of the dirty water. The size of the big claws on it boy! He's a mean old sonofabitch.

>(HUMPY *examines the crab mark on his arm*.)

ZAK Can I talk to yeh for a minute Sonia?

SONIA What about?

ZAK What do yeh think?

SONIA Tch . . . There's no point, Zak. I mean forget it!

ZAK Why though, Sonia, that's all I'm wantin' to know. Why?

SONIA Why? Yeh two timed on me every chance yeh got Zak. And you were turnin' up drunk all

	the time. And late. And the way yeh talk to me.
Zak	What do yeh mean?
Sonia	Yeh talk to me as if I was one of the boys or somethin'. I'm not one of the boys Zak. I'm a girl, a woman. Talk to Broaders like that if yeh want but not to me.
Zak	What do yeh mean the way I talk to yeh like?
Sonia	Cursin' all the time and all. And puckin' me in the shoulder all the time. Yeh don't know how to treat a girl, Zak. Yeh haven't a clue how to treat a girl. Anyway I'm goin' out with Brian now so . . . What's so funny? Do yeh think that I'm not good enough for him or somethin'?
Zak	I never said that.
Sonia	Well what then?
Zak	He's just not your type, that's all.
Sonia	What do yeh mean?
Zak	For God's sake Sonia he's a nancy boy in an office.
Sonia	Yeah and I'm just a scrubber in a factory, is that it?
Zak	He's a nancy boy in an office. I'd bate him with me hand tied behind me back. Do yeh think I wouldn't? Get him out here then. Go ahead.
Sonia	Goodbye Zak.
Zak	Get him out here.

SONIA	I'd like to eat my lunch in peace if yeh don't mind.
ZAK	What? Yeah, right (*He storms off back to the boys.*)
HUMPY	Yes, he's a mean old mother. A mean old mother of mine.
	(BROADERS *look into* ZAK'S *eyes.* ZAK *shakes his head.*)
BROADERS	That one's gettin' too high and mighty for herself if yeh ask me . . . (*Shouts.*) . . . Like her brother! (SONIA *leaves in a huff.*)
HUMPY	If you're too broken-hearted to eat all your sandwiches Zak, I'll give yeh a hand if yeh like.
ZAK	Fuck off Humpy, will yeh.
	(*Pause.*)
DRIBBLER	This is a right little picnic we're havin' here now Bridie, ain't it? Hah? It reminds me of all the times we used to come here to pick the fruit when we were young, do yeh remember? You used to have more strawberries on your face now than yeh ever put in your basket. And I used to have to top up your can for yeh all the time so you'd make enough money to go to the pictures. Jaysus this was a beautiful place then though lads, I'm not coddin' yeh. Menapia Mansion!
HUMPY	Where was that, Dribbler?
DRIBBLER	I'll tell yeh now exactly where it was Humpy. Do yeh know the auld packin' shed around back there?
HUMPY	Yeah.

DRIBBLER	Well that used to be Menapia Mansion. I know you'd never think it to look at it now but that used to be a stunnin' place one time boy. Auld Taylor built it in his heyday. And all these gardens were all landscaped and all. It was a beautiful place alright Bridie was it?
BRIDIE	Yeah. It was. All the roses growin' down by the river. And the lilac on the orchard wall. Pear trees and peaches and plums and apples. And tomatoes growin' in the greenhouse. And the beautiful gardens! God it'd do your heart good just to walk past here in the mornin's. And comin' home from a dance at night all the boys and girls'd always cut through here for a short cut and it seemed to be summer all the time that time. The smell of the sea minglin' with the smell of the summer. The water used to be like glass, as clear as crystal - and when me mother'd be makin' the tea she'd send me out to see if there was any sign of me Da yet and I'd go out onto the bank and I'd see all the little boats comin' over the horizon - thirty or forty of them. All the men comin' home for their tea . . . Yeh could swim off of that auld beach then. Yeh couldn't do it now, yeh'd never know what you'd catch out of it.
DRIBBLER	And we all thought it'd never end Bridie, hah! (*He looks at her and smiles.*)
BRIDIE	Mmn. The lonely auld shell of the summer!
	(BROADERS *takes out his catapult and fires at something.*)
HUMPY	Nice one Broaders.
	(HUMPY *runs offstage and begins thrashing something to death with a stone, re-entering with the bloody carcass of a dead seagull.*)
	What will I do with it Broaders?

BROADERS	Give it to Zak there.
HUMPY	What? Yeah, right. Here y'are Zak, put that between your bread boy.

(HUMPY *throws the seagull at* ZAK *and laughs.* ZAK, *in a rage, picks up the dead bird and chases* HUMPY *off stage.* BROADERS *follows them. Lights down. Lights rise on the kitchen.* DRIBBLER *and* EAGLE *are sitting at the table drinking mugs of tea.* ISAAC *is squatting on the floor, polishing his shoes.* VERONICA *is at the sink. It is night time.*)

DRIBBLER   Yeh know what way you're fixed with a good cowboy book though lads yeh know. Yeh know who's who and what's what and who's right and who's wrong and all the rest of it. I mean to say it has everything - action, scenery, romance. Yeh know the prairies and the mountains and all that kind of stuff. Louis L'Amour, Eagle! A great writer boy! Did yeh ever read anythin' by him, no? Well I must have read nearly everything that fella ever wrote boy. "River's West", "A Man Called Noon", "Heller With A Gun", "Lando". The whole shebang boy! Mastermind! The Life And Works Of Louis L'Amour! There's one of the best cowboy books I ever read though lads. "Duel In The Sun". It was written by a fella called Chris Mortimer. Accordin' to the blurb he only wrote the one book and then he was killed tragically - shot through the head by his jilted lover when she found him in the arms of another woman. She emptied her revolver into him. Classic stuff! It's a pity he didn't live to tell the tale says you, he could have had a best-seller on his hands.

ISAAC   What's it about, Dribbler?

DRIBBLER   "Duel in The Sun"? It tells the story of this auld agin' gunslinger who decided to hang up

	his guns and settle down in a little one-horse town. Half the book shows yeh the auld fella goin' about his business in the small town while the other half tells yeh all about this young punk of a gunslinger who's wantin' to make a name for himself by takin' on the auld lad . . .
VERONICA	How much did yeh get for the salmon after?
EAGLE	Forty three quid.
VERONICA	Where is it?
EAGLE	I have it here. Well I have twenty quid of it. I had to pay for the wood for the hut out of it yeh see.
VERONICA	What?
DRIBBLER	. . . Well your man goes though hell and high water to get to the little town, I'm not coddin' yeh - through the Badlands of New Mexico, through Indian country and everything - drawn towards his destiny as your man puts it . . .
VERONICA	But sure there's lashin's of auld wood out the back there that yeh could have used for it instead of . . .
EAGLE	I have used some of it. But I needed special timber for the hut yeh see. Wooden pilin's and that. I mean to say it all has to be tied together like yeh know.
VERONICA	Sonia and young Taylor were up here with me this evenin' Eagle and I had nothin' to give them. I hadn't a bloody biscuit in the . . .
DRIBBLER	. . . Meanwhile, the auld fella seems to sense that there's trouble brewin' and every day at noon . . .

VERONICA	. . . house and now you tell me that you're after spendin' twenty three pounds on wood for an auld hut that'll be burnt down tomorrow mornin'.
DRIBBLER	. . . he straps on his holster again and stands on the veranda of the saloon, lookin' down the street . . .
EAGLE	The hut has to be built in a certain way. It's a tradition.
VERONICA	Yeah well we have a tradition in this house too Eagle like yeh know. When the rent is paid and there's plenty of food on the table then we're entitled to play our little games.
EAGLE	What are yeh talkin' about - playin' games? Hah? What are yeh talkin' about?

(DRIBBLER *has fallen silent.*)

VERONICA	You know well enough what I'm talkin' about Eagle. There's a job goin' over in that auld factory and you didn't even bother your arse goin' to see about it. I wouldn't mind but yeh promised me that if things didn't pick up soon you'd . . .
EAGLE	Things did pick up. I caught two salmon didn't I?
VERONICA	Yeah and yeh spent more than half the money on an auld hut that'll be burnt down tomorrow mornin'.
EAGLE	Lord Jaysus ain't that awful Dribbler, what I've to listen to too, ain't it? Hah? I mean just because a man loves what he's doin', what he's born to do, they're all down on him. I don't know . . . I mean I don't know what else I'm supposed to do anyway. What am I supposed to do? I have me nets all over the place - I've lobster pots out by the Black

	Man, I've eel traps out on Useless Island, me salmon nets are up the river and I've a rake of crab boxes all over the place. I go out diggin' bait every chance I get. I mean . . . What am I supposed to do!
VERONICA	We're in trouble here Eagle yeh know. The cupboard is bare boy!
DRIBBLER	But sure the hut has to be built in a certain way Veronica like yeh know - a certain shape to it and that.

(VERONICA *throws* DRIBBLER *a dirty look and turns away. Pause.*)

ISAAC	What happened after Dribbler? Did the young fella kill the auld lad?
DRIBBLER	What? No the auld lad knackered him alright.
ISAAC	How come?

(VERONICA *takes out a little mirror to check her appearance.* EAGLE *watches her jealously.*)

DRIBBLER	He just stood on the veranda in the shade and let the young fella come to him. The young lad walked up the deserted street, two guns on him, hangin' low down, a black hat on his head tied under his chin . . .
EAGLE	Where are yeh goin'?
DRIBBLER	. . . He was in the shade too until he came to the mouth of this little alleyway . . .
VERONICA	The Railway Hotel.
DRIBBLER	. . . And then the noon day sun came blastin' over the roof tops into his eyes, blindin' him . . .
VERONICA	School committee meetin'.

DRIBBLER   . . . And that's when the auld lad made his move . . .

EAGLE   In the Railway Hotel! How come it's not in the school?

DRIBBLER   . . . As soon as the young fella squinted the auld lad reached for his holster and gunned him down.

VERONICA   I don't know. The heatin' is off or somethin'.

DRIBBLER   Cute yeh see. "Duel in the Sun"!

(DRIBBLER *struts like a gunslinger.* ISAAC *stands to face him.* DRIBBLER *goes for his imaginary guns.* ISAAC *beats him to the draw.* DRIBBLER *falls to the floor.* ISAAC *puts his imaginary gun away. Suddenly* DRIBBLER *sits up and goes for his guns again.* ISAAC *draws and empties his gun into him.* DRIBBLER *dies.* ISAAC *goes to him.* DRIBBLER *grabs his leg.* ISAAC *goes for his gun again.*)

DRIBBLER   You've no bullets left.

(ISAAC *takes out an imaginary knife and stabs* DRIBBLER *with it many times.* DRIBBLER *dies, painfully, slowly, kicking. Then he sits up.*)

Are you wantin' to go for a pint or what Eagle?

(EAGLE *is jealously watching* VERONICA's *transformation.*)

EAGLE   What? Yeah, might as well I suppose.

DRIBBLER   Right. Hang on then 'til I go to the toilet . . .

(DRIBBLER *rises and makes to leave.* ISAAC *is watching him like a hawk.* DRIBBLER *turns in the doorway and goes for his guns.* ISAAC *throws his imaginary knife.* DRIBBLER *pretends to be hit in the neck and falls to the floor, moaning and choking and out of sight. He exits, whistling.* ISAAC *hides down behind the table in ambush.*)

VERONICA (*putting on her coat*) Isaac, you look after the place until I come back won't yeh?

ISAAC Yeah right . . . Dribbler is a right bit of a laugh Ma, ain't he?

VERONICA Yeah. Hilarious!

(*She leaves. Pause. Lights down. Lights rise.* BRIDIE *is sitting on a trolley in front of the factory gates.* ZAK, BROADERS *and* HUMPY *enter.*)

BROADERS Oon Bridie boy!

HUMPY Hey Bridie, Dribbler is up in the pub lookin' for you yeh know.

BRIDIE Is he?

BROADERS Don't mind him Bridie. You stay where yeh are hon. That fella is only wantin' to throw a rake of drink into yeh so he can take advantage of yeh . . . Give us a kiss, I wants to be sick. (*He leans on her.*)

BRIDIE Get away from me yeh little animal yeh.

BROADERS Ah I'm only jokin' yeh Bridie. Bridie!

HUMPY Yeh sang well tonight Bridie, fair play to yeh. (*He sings, almost monotone.*) I let my hair down, I slipped my shoes off, danced like an angel . . .

BROADERS You should learn to sing a different song Bridie. People don't like listenin' to someone

	singin' the same auld song all the time yeh know.
HUMPY	We'll have to write one for her Broaders.
BROADERS	Yeah. (*He sings.*) Oh I am the village bicycle And they come from miles around; To ride me up and down this cosy little town; Oh hurry up kind sir, hurry up kind sir says she, For the angelus is ringing and I must go home for tea . . .
HUMPY	(*laughs and sings*) I let my drawers down, I slipped me knickers off . . . Do yeh think we belong on the stage Bridie?
BRIDIE	Yeah, sweepin' it!
BROADERS	Hey Bridie, would yeh able to fix Humpy here up with that new one that started in the factory the other day there?
HUMPY	You shut up Broaders.
BROADERS	What's her name? Anita?
HUMPY	Don't mind him Bridie.
BROADERS	Just tell her that if she agrees to go out with him we'll all chip in and buy her a guide dog.
HUMPY	Very funny Broaders.
	(BROADERS *laughs. He runs to the gates and begins shaking them furiously.*)
BROADERS	Let me in, let me in. I wants to go to work. I'm addicted to it. Let me in . . . Please!
	(HUMPY *looks at him and laughs.*)

HUMPY	What age is she anyway Bridie?
BRIDIE	Who?
HUMPY	Anita?
BRIDIE	She's old enough to have more sense than to go out with a gobshite like you.
HUMPY	What?

(BRIDIE *throws him a dirty look.* HUMPY *backs away.* BROADERS *sniggers and looks across at* ZAK *sitting on top of a pile of mussel sacks, gazing wistfully into space.*)

BROADERS	Oh to be in love hah! Were yeh ever in love Bridie? No! . . . Neither was I. Not accordin' to that anyway. (*Nodding towards* ZAK.) Oh! Speakin' of love!

(SONIA *and* BRIAN *enter.*)

BRIAN	Have you fellas no homes to go to? . . . How are yeh lads.
HUMPY	How's it goin'?
BRIAN	How are yeh Bridie?
BRIDIE	How are yeh.
BROADERS	Must have forgot his spectacles lads.
BRIAN	(*opening the lock on the gates*) What's that?
BROADERS	I say did yeh forget somethin' yeah?
BRIAN	Somethin' like that.
SONIA	I'll hang on here for yeh Brian.
BRIAN	Right. I won't be a minute. (*He exits.*)

SONIA: How are yeh Bridie? Are yeh alright?

BRIDIE: I came out here for a bit of peace and quiet. I picked a right spot for it didn't I? Where did yeh go to?

SONIA: We went down to the Railway Hotel. We just had a few drinks that's all.

BROADERS: Did yeh sit up at the bar or was it waiter service? Hey Sonia, what's goin' on here anyway? I hope this fella is not knockin' off the factory on the sly now or anythin'. The culprit was apprehended comin' out of the factory gates with a pocket full of mussels and a mouthful of lobster. He had a big slippery eel down the front of his trousers and a sack of mussels stuffed up the back of his jumper. When asked to identify himself he answered to the name of Humpy O'Brien.

HUMPY: Hey Broaders, watch it.

BROADERS: To further disguise himself he had to whip off one of his ears, cut out one of his eyes, spit out a handful of teeth and grow a mangy auld beard down one side of his face but even still the police sergeant could see that he was far too good lookin' to be the man he claimed to be.

HUMPY: Very funny Broaders, tell me when to laugh.

BROADERS: Cut off his testicles someone said. No, no, his girlfriend cried, they're mine, all mine.

SONIA: Do yeh know somethin' Broaders but you really should try washin' yourself sometime because there's an awful smell of fish off of yeh, yeh know.

BROADERS: And what do yeh think you smell of, eau de cologne or some fuckin' thing?

HUMPY	(*laughing*) Broaders is ragin'. Yeh see Broaders it doesn't matter how smart yeh think yeh are you'll still get your come-uppence sooner or later boy. Yeh could be the smartest lad in the world but you'll always meet someone who's smarter than yeh.
	(BROADERS *shakes his head and sighs. He goes to* ZAK.)
BROADERS	Yes, oh to be in love!
ZAK	What?
BROADERS	Here he is now . . . (BRIAN *is returning.*) The walk of him! (*They laugh.*) . . . Is everything alright in there yeh?
BRIAN	(*locking up*) Yeah.
BROADERS	That's good . . . Hey, where are you from anyway, the city?
BRIAN	Yeah.
BROADERS	So how come yeh came to be so well up on the dirty little world of the slippery auld eel then? Did yeh go to college and read up on it or somethin' yeah?
BRIAN	That's right.
BROADERS	For how long?
BRIAN	Three years.
BROADERS	Three years! Jasus, you should have come out with me. I could have taught yeh all yeh needed to know in a fortnight. Mind you yeh need to have the stomach for it. The auld trawler is inclined to be a bit bumpy at times like yeh know.

BRIAN	Oh I think I'd've managed alright Broaders, don't worry about that.
BROADERS	What? Oh that's right, sure you're a bit of a deep sea diver ain't yeh? I forgot all about that. Yeah! Jacques Cousteau the Second, hah! Not like you and me, Humpy - divin' off the shelter wall in the summer.
HUMPY	Yeah or walkin' the greasy pole during the regatta.

(*Pause.*)

BROADERS	So, what do yeh think of the place anyway?
BRIAN	Grand. Great really. Good people. Great stories to tell. Everywhere I go nearly I hear a different story - about the Dempsey Twins and that. Dribbler was tellin' me that one this mornin' there.
BROADERS	Yeah well I wouldn't pay much attention to all of that if I was you. Up around here they'll only tell yeh what they think yeh want to hear.
BRIAN	Ah no, they were genuine stories alright. I find all that stuff interestin' anyway. I mean to say the history of this area is probably bound up in all those little stories yeh know.
HUMPY	By Jaysus and we could tell yeh some hairy stories I don't mind tellin' yeh. Couldn't we lads? Zak, do yeh remember the night we went to the dance in Enniscorthy? (*He laughs.*)
BRIAN	Oh I dare say Humpy the day'll come when your name'll be trippin' off the tips of the tongues of people who are not even born yet boy!
BROADERS	I gravely doubt that somehow or other.

BRIAN	Ah well yeh see people don't always realise that they're livin' interestin' lives yeh know.
	(BROADERS *scoffs*.)
SONIA	I think what Brian means is that . . .
BROADERS	I know what he means.
	(*Silence*.)
BRIAN	We'll go Sonia. I'll see yeh in the mornin' lads.
HUMPY	Yeah right.
BRIAN	Goodbye Bridie.
BRIDIE	Goodnight.
SONIA	I'll see yeh Bridie.
BRIDIE	See yeh Sonia.
BROADERS	All the best . . . Try and get in on time in the mornin' if yeh can will yeh.
	(SONIA *and* BRIAN *leave*.)
HUMPY	Come on and we'll follow them Broaders will we, see what they're up to. Come on. I'm goin' to follow them. Come on. Are yeh comin' Zak. Come on . . .
	(HUMPY *exits. Pause.* BROADERS *goes to* BRIDIE. *He gazes up at the starry sky*.)
BROADERS	There's no one out there yeh know Bridie.
BRIDIE	What?
BROADERS	There's no one out there. There's no one watchin' over us or anythin'. Nobody's

keepin' tabs on all the things we do and say to one another. And do yeh know what that means Bridie? It means we can do what we want. We can say what we like. Because there's no one out there. Nobody gives a shit! Here, wait 'til I show yeh this. (*He takes out a knife.*) Do yeh see this? Do yeh see that big crab that's welded into the blade there? Here go on, take it. Do yeh see that big crab? Well he's sort of my hero yeh know. Yeah. That fella crawls out of the muddy waters every day of his workin' life and he sets off in a straight line devourin' everythin' he sees. He don't give no one nothin'. He just takes what he wants and leaves the rest behind him. And right, you may say to me that at any time any one of us could just step on him and crush him to death and that'd be that but that's not the point. While he's alive, as long as he exists, he's the kingpin around here. He's the one who rules the roost. And that's the reason. That's why he's my hero. (*He takes the knife back.*) And he don't need to tell no stories either Bridie. And he don't need to listen to them. And do yeh know somethin'? Neither do I . . . No, there's no one out there.

(BROADERS *exits. Pause.*)

ZAK	Would yeh be able to put a word in with Sonia for me Bridie?
BRIDIE	What?
ZAK	Would yeh be able to put a word in with her for me?
BRIDIE	How do yeh mean? I mean what do yeh want me to say to her?
ZAK	I don't know. Just put a word in for me like.
BRIDIE	Look Zak, why don't yeh just let her go now. You're a good lookin' fella. You could have

	lashin's of girls after yeh. Let her go. Sonia has a chance of gettin' out of here now so why not let her take it?
Zak	What do yeh mean?
	(BRIDIE *sighs, looks into his eyes and runs her fingers gently through his hair.*)
BRIDIE	You are a good lookin' fella yeh know. Yeh remind me of a boy I used to know one time. He was a bit wild too and all mixed up on the inside just like you are now. I had a baby for him . . . But unfortunately he was just about to get married to someone else when it all began. For three solid weeks I met him every night in the little graveyard beyond here. It was probably just a last wild fling as far as he was concerned but I fell hook, line and sinker for him. I swear I've never met anyone like him before or since. And God knows I've looked . . . I never told anyone who the father was. I never let the cat out of the bag on him. I don't think he even realised it himself to tell yeh the truth. Well if he did he never acknowledged it anyway, let's put it that way . . . It was a baby boy - stillborn. We buried him in a little overgrown grave with a wooden cross to mark the spot. Me Da painted the child's name on it but the rain came that night and washed it away . . . If he had've lived he would have been thirteen tomorrow - the tenth of November, St Martin's Eve - and I'd be singin' a different song today than the one I'm, singin' now . . . Let her go Zak. I know it's hard but sometimes when yeh love someone yeh just have to let them go.
Zak	I can't Bridie. Me heart is sort of set on her yeh see. Yeh might put in a word for me if yeh get a chance will yeh.

(Zak *leaves. Lights down. Lights rise.* Brian *and* Sonia *are sitting together in the little graveyard.*)

BRIAN (*reading from the diary*) Here it is. Listen to this. 'Saw her today for the very first time - a magnificent lookin' woman with a mane of coal black hair and a pair of fiery eyes. Like a magnet she drew me towards her. She had come to sell me a bucketful of the loveliest looking oysters that I have ever seen. I asked her where she had found them and she offered to show me the place tomorrow. I met her . . .' I don't know what that is. I can't make it out. 'She led me across the rocks on the far side of Useless Island and just opposite the . . .' What's that?

SONIA The Black Man. The old marker in the middle of the harbour.

BRIAN '. . . just opposite the Black Man we . . .' something, something . . . 'I was not thinking of oysters. My mind was elsewhere. She smelt of the sea. Everything about her - her hair, her face, her hands, her breath even. She was like a creature that had risen up out of the sea to come and live amongst us. I wanted to throw myself down at her feet. I wanted to live inside of her . . . ' I can't believe this. I mean, I remember me grandfather as a real cranky old man with hardly anything to say for himself. We used to come here as children for the summer holidays and I swear he never put any pass on us at all. He used to lock himself away in a dark room - poutin' lips and smellin' of whisky. We were all afraid of our lives of him and here he is cavorting with a married woman.

SONIA He sounds like a fairly passionate man then.

BRIAN He does, doesn't he?

SONIA	I wonder who she is. Does it say who she is? (BRIAN *shakes his head.*) When was all this supposed to have happened anyway?
BRIAN	Oh I don't know. Forty years ago nearly.
SONIA	Read some more.
BRIAN	(*chuckles, kisses her and reads*) 'Today I plucked up the courage to venture to kiss her. She responded to me. I took her in my arms.' This is incredible! . . . 'I took her in my arms . . .' I can't make out the rest of that page. It's all smudged. Just as well I think. But wait 'til yeh hear this. 'Stole away last night to Useless Island for another night of bliss.' Another night of it if yeh don't mind! And here's the best part. 'We had a close shave when her husband passed not four feet from where we lay. She shivered in my arms with the fright and I had to comfort her.' . . . Jesus! (BRIAN *shakes his head and chuckles nervously.*)
SONIA	I wonder if they ever came up here.
BRIAN	They probably did. They probably sat right here where we're sittin' now. And then she laid back in the long grass.
SONIA	Here?
BRIAN	Yeah.
SONIA	Yeah?
	(*Slight pause.* BRIAN *rises and goes to her. He takes her in his arms. They kiss, slumping onto the ground. Suddenly she stops him, gazing off into the distance.*)
BRIAN	What's up?
SONIA	Humpy O'Brien is watchin' us.

BRIAN	What? Where?
SONIA	Over there by the gate. Do yeh see him? Tch, he's an awful ejit that fella is . . . Come on, we'd better get out of here Brian, or he'll have it all over the place.
BRIAN	What?
SONIA	Come on.

(SONIA *rises and straightens her attire.* BRIAN *does likewise. They leave.* HUMPY *enters, hiding behind the tree and running from grave to grave. He finds the diary that* BRIAN *has left behind. He pockets it as* BROADERS *enters.*)

HUMPY	Ah yeh missed it Broaders boy.
BROADERS	What?
HUMPY	She was lyin' down there with him and everythin' Broaders. Yeh missed it boy!
BROADERS	How do yeh know?
HUMPY	Because I was watchin' them. The pair of them were sittin' down here where they thought they couldn't be seen. He got her down onto the ground then and she started atin' the face off of him and everythin' boy. It bet the bun altogether here so it did. She's some bitch though ain't she? Hah? Zak'll go mad boy. Right beside your granny's grave too Broaders hah! No respect boy! I'm goin' to tell yeh one thing too but I wouldn't say she's the first girl to come up here with that fella either since he arrived would you? I'd say that lad's a real whoremaster altogether goin' around would you? Hah?
BROADERS	That's for sure. He's makin' whores out of the whole lot of us here as far as I can see.

HUMPY	How do yeh mean?
BROADERS	But sure he has us all where he wants us now hasn't he? Clockin' in and out of that place for him every day. Luggin' and draggin' and sweepin' floors and all the rest of it. No matter where we're workin' yeh know he can see us out of his office window. It doesn't matter where we are - out in the auld trawler or unloadin' on the shore or down in the shelter - it makes no odds, he can see us. And he's always watchin' too - always lookin' and checkin'. We're just dirt under his fingernails, that's all we are to him. Dirt boy. We're no better than the auld crabs and eels that we have to catch for him. Dirt!
HUMPY	That's a fact alright. Did yeh ever see the way he looks at yeh. He has a real dirty eye hasn't he? Your name'll be trippin' off the tips of their tongues says he! The voice on him! We're just dirt under his fingernails boy. Yes, whores he's after makin' of the whole lot of us here ain't he? Hah?
BROADERS	Yeah. I'm afraid so.
HUMPY	The whoremaster anyway. (*Shouts.*) WHOREMASTER!

(HUMPY *hides down out of sight.* BROADERS *just stands there.*)

HUMPY	Get down Broaders. Get down will yeh. Broaders! He's watchin'. He's lookin'. He'll see yeh Broaders!

(BROADERS *stands staring off into the distance. Lights down. Lights rise on the kitchen. It is the following night.* SONIA *is packing stuff into a cardboard box.* MOSEY *is sitting, smoking, a few boxes at his feet.* VERONICA *and* ISAAC *arrive with more boxes - all the stuff for*

ACT ONE

ISAAC's *trip, blankets and sleeping bags, food and hot water bottles, etc.*)

VERONICA Where's Eagle?

MOSEY He's just gone down to the boat for a minute. He said you were all to wait here for him.

VERONICA Right. Have you got a packet of tea bags there Sonia?

SONIA Yeah, they're here look.

VERONICA Give them to me will yeh. I'm wantin' to keep all the food stuff together if I can. Here, put those toilet rolls in your box Sonia. All the food stuff is in this little box here Isaac, look.

ISAAC Right. (ISAAC *is writing in his diary.*)

VERONICA Tell your Daddy that I put a few firelighters in this brown bag here.

ISAAC (*writing*) Right.

VERONICA Were my eyes deceivin' me or did I see Humpy O'Brien goin' by my window tonight with a girl?

SONIA Yeah. The boys fixed him up with this new one that started in the factory.

VERONICA God she must have no one belongin' to her then to go out with him.

SONIA Did yeh see the state of the suit on him. He's like somethin' the cat dragged in ain't he? (*They laugh.*)

ISAAC What date is this Ma?

VERONICA What? St Martin's Eve - the tenth of November.

SONIA	What are yeh doin', Isaac?
ISAAC	I'm writin' it all into me diary.
SONIA	I never knew you kept a diary.
ISAAC	I only got it today sure.
VERONICA	Bridgey Malloy sent yeh over a cake too, Isaac. Look.
ISAAC	Yeah I know.
VERONICA	Yeh should feel the weight of it, Sonia. It's like an anchor so it is. I don't know what the hell she puts in it at all.
ISAAC	Is this alright Sonia? Today's the day that I go out to the island. I can't wait to see my little hut. Bridgey Malloy sent me over a cake and Mosey Brennan gave me a medal.
VERONICA	Who is that anyway Mosey - St Christopher?
MOSEY	St Martin.
ISAAC	(*writing*) St Martin.
VERONICA	I'd say that's fairly old Mosey, is it?
MOSEY	Yeah, it's fairly old alright.
ISAAC	And me Aunty Sonia said she'd give me a pound if I come back alive.

(SONIA *chuckles*.)

SONIA	That's great Isaac. You should write down everything that happens to yeh tonight now.
ISAAC	That's what I'm goin' to do sure.

SONIA	It's a strange auld habit ain't it? Keepin' a diary?
VERONICA	Mmn . . . I kept one yeh know.
SONIA	Yeah?
VERONICA	Yeah. When I was about fifteen I kept a diary. The first day I saw Eagle I went home and wrote it all down in it. He was down in the shelter stripped to the waist and he paintin' an auld boat or somethin'. I was goin' out with him practically the next week. It's amazin' what yeh can do when yeh set your mind to it too ain't it? (*Both women laugh.*)
SONIA	What do you think Mosey. Do yeh think Isaac should write it all down tonight?
MOSEY	What? Oh yeah . . . As long as he spells my name right of course!
ISAAC	M O S E Y. Mosey.

(EAGLE *enters.*)

EAGLE	Alright lads? Is everythin' nearly ready yeah?
VERONICA	Yeah.
ISAAC	I'm bringin' me diary out to the island with me Da.
EAGLE	Yeah? That's good. There's a good crowd down there mind yeh Mosey.
MOSEY	Aye?
EAGLE	Did yeh hear that Isaac, there's a good crowd down there to see yeh off boy. You've packed enough stuff for him anyway Veronica. Anyone'd think he was goin' out for a month or somethin'.

VERONICA	Better to be sure than sorry. (*She is helping* ISAAC *into a big hooded anorak.*) Yeh stuck in those few extra blankets for him Sonia didn't yeh?
SONIA	Yeah.
EAGLE	He won't need all that stuff Veronica. Sure I'm after buildin' him a hut out there man and it's like a little igloo so it is.
VERONICA	What do yeh think the child is, an eskimo or somethin'?
ISAAC	I'm goin' to tell yeh one thing but I feel like a feckin' Eskimo in this thing.
VERONICA	You stop that cursin' boy.
MOSEY	I threw an auld ground sheet into the end of the boat for yeh Eagle. Keep out some of the damp.
EAGLE	Oh thanks Mosey. Although I'm after buildin' him a sort of a bed in it to raise him up off of the ground.
MOSEY	So I heard. Jaysus it's a wonder you didn't put a lav and everythin' in it and yeh at it.
EAGLE	Modern times, Mosey . . . We may make two trips down to the boat Isaac I think.
VERONICA	Yeh won't need to make two trips at all. Meself and Sonia'll give yeh a hand.
EAGLE	Alright then, come on, let's go.
MOSEY	Are you rowing out or what?
EAGLE	No. Sail.

VERONICA	Now you remember what I was sayin' to yeh Isaac, and stay well clear of that fire once your Daddy is gone home, do yeh hear me?
ISAAC	Yeah.
VERONICA	Eagle, you won't light that fire too close to the hut now sure yeh won't?
EAGLE	No.
VERONICA	And stay clear of the water's edge too hon' won't yeh? I've an awful fear of him fallin' into the water, Sonia.
SONIA	Oh he'll be alright Veronica.
ISAAC	With this big bloody thing on me I'll probably float anyway. (*The women chuckle.*) If you're wantin' to kiss me now or anythin' Ma I'd advise yeh to do it now because there's no way you're doin' it down there in front of everyone.
VERONICA	Ain't that awful Sonia?

(VERONICA *puts her arms around him and hugs and kisses him.* SONIA *does likewise.* EAGLE *picks up a box and makes to leave.*)

EAGLE	Whenever yez are ready now!

(*They leave,* ISAAC *doubling back for his diary. Lights down. Lights rise on the graveyard.* BROADERS *is standing over a grave.* ZAK *is sitting beneath the tree, gazing out to sea.*)

ZAK	Maybe we should have gone down to see him off hah?
BROADERS	What for?

ZAK	Ah I don't know. It feels kind of queer to find yourself on the outside lookin' in don't it?
BROADERS	Not if that's where yeh want to be.
ZAK	Like Eagle yeh mean?
BROADERS	Do me a favour will yeh.

(BROADERS *turns away.* ZAK *watches him.* VERONICA *enters.*)

VERONICA	Any sign of them Zak?
ZAK	Yeah, they're just goin' round by the Black Man now. There. Can yeh see them? They're nearly out there now sure . . . He had a fair auld send off after anyway didn't he?
VERONICA	Yeah. (*She looks at* BROADERS.) Sayin' a few prayers for his granny is he?
ZAK	Yeah.
VERONICA	Poor Marian. God all the times I went across to tell her me troubles. She was one great bit of stuff so she was. Sure poor Mosey is lost without her. And she was the only one who was ever able to get any good of that young lad . . . Thumbelina knows her way around.
ZAK	What?
VERONICA	Ah it was an auld sayin' of hers. She'd be watchin' a race on the telly or somethin' and her horse'd maybe just barely nick it be a nose. 'I told yez', she'd say. 'Of course yeh wouldn't listen to me. Oh Thumbelina knows her way around boy!' Jaysus even in these surroundin's she looked like a queen . . . Sometimes yeh have to wonder what it's all about Zak, don't yeh. Yeh live and yeh die and then they put yeh down a big hole to rot. Sure no wonder people go to so much trouble

to put their mark on the world while they're here.

(*She looks out to sea apprehensively.*)

HUMPY   (*entering*) I'm goin' to tell yeh one thing Zak but she's some snobby bitch boy . . . Hello Missus. Do yeh know where she wanted to go Zak? The Railway Hotel! Says I to her, 'If the Shark public house is not good enough for you then you can say goodbye to me here and now and be done with it.'

ZAK   And what did she say?

HUMPY   She said 'Good riddance to bad rubbish', and she walked away. 'Ha ha', says I to her, 'tickle me under the arm and call me Geronimo.' . . . Any sign of them?

ZAK   They're out around the Black Man.

HUMPY   Broaders sayin' hello to his granny again is he?

ZAK   Yeah.

VERONICA   He was dyin' alive about her wasn't he?

HUMPY   That's for sure. That was the only time I ever saw him cryin' yeh know - at her funeral. Do yeh remember Zak? The big red eyes on him? (*He chuckles.*) Here lies the body of Marian Brennan who gave herself to the sea on the ninth of November nineteen hundred and eighty four . . . She's alright there though Missus, buried nearly next door to me Da there she is.

VERONICA   They keep the grave lovely anyway.

HUMPY   Broaders looks after that himself yeh know Missus - fair play to him. I'm goin' to tell yeh one thing but it's a pity Bridie wouldn't do the same with this one here. The state of it!

	She comes up here every Sunday yeh know and stands over this auld grave for hours on end, mutterin' to herself. It'd match her better to clean it up a bit wouldn't it. Put a bit of paint on it or somethin'. Look at the state of it! Yeh can't read the writin' on the little cross nor nothin' . . . Little Jimmy O'Keefe the baker was on his way to work the mornin' Broaders' granny drown herself yeh know. He said he saw her goin' down the bank - all dressed up like a dog's dinner - and then she walked out into the water the same as if she was goin' down the town. The man nearly died with the fright boy! But sure auld Mosey is still not right yeh know . . . Queer though ain't it?
VERONICA	Mmn . . .
HUMPY	(*brushing back the briars and weeds from the little headstone*) St Martin's Eve 1978. Bridie's little bambino hah! (*He chuckles.*)
	(*Slight pause.*)
VERONICA	(*going*) I'll see yeh lads.
ZAK	Yeah, right Veronica.
HUMPY	All the best Missus (*She goes.*) . . . Someone was tellin' me that she was seen down in the bar of the Railway Hotel last night drinkin' with your man Collins the teacher.
ZAK	No chance!
HUMPY	(*sings*) Oh I am the village bicycle, And they come from miles around . . . (*Taking out the diary.*) Hey Broaders, when is a secret not a secret? . . . When everybody knows about it! (*He laughs.*) . . . Wait 'til yeh hear this. 'Saw her today for the very first

time - a magnificent looking woman with a mane of coal black hair and a pair of fiery eyes. Like a magnet she drew me towards her. She came to sell me a bucket of the loveliest lookin' oysters I've ever seen . . .'

(*Lights down. Lights rise.* EAGLE *and* ISAAC *are out in the boat, travelling beneath a starry sky, the lights of the town behind them in the distance.*)

ISAAC   Sure there's no such thing as wild boars in this country any more Da, is there?

EAGLE   No.

ISAAC   I knew that. Humpy O'Brien was tryin' to tell me that he came out here one day last week and found all this wild boar shit all over the place.

EAGLE   Don't mind him. Sure St Patrick drove the wild boars out of here years ago son.

ISAAC   St Patrick drove the snakes out of Ireland Da, not the wild boars.

EAGLE   Who told yeh that?

ISAAC   The teacher.

EAGLE   Yeah well he drove the wild boars out as well. And he told them all that they could take their shite with them when they were goin'.

(ISAAC *ponders.*)

ISAAC   Well if there's no wild boars here any more where did all the manure come from out on the island?

EAGLE   It was probably that auld pig that escaped from the bacon factory a few weeks ago there.

ISAAC	What did it do Da, swim out there or somethin'?
EAGLE	Yeah, it swam out there.
ISAAC	And is it still out there would yeh say?
EAGLE	No. To tell yeh the truth Isaac, he got so browned off out there that he swam back and gave himself up.
ISAAC	Our teacher was tellin' us that a pig can't swim very far without cuttin' his own throat yeh know. He swims like this, Da. Kind of like a dog's paddle.
EAGLE	Isaac, will you sit still in the boat before yeh have the pair of us in the water.
ISAAC	It's nails are so sharp that he ends up cuttin' his own throat. (*He runs his nails across* EAGLE's *throat.*) Ahh . . .
EAGLE	Jaysus that teacher of yours is a mine of information alright ain't he?
ISAAC	Yeah he knows everything boy . . . Hey Da did the pig that escaped from the bacon factory end up cuttin' it's own throat would yeh say?
EAGLE	No, he got back alright.
ISAAC	How come? I mean to say that's a fair auld distance for a pig to swim without cuttin' it's own throat ain't it?
EAGLE	Yeah well yeh see Isaac, this lad wasn't doin' the dog's paddle like yeh know. This fella was able to do the breast stroke.

(*Pause.*)

ISAAC	Look at all the stars Da. Kind of electric stars. Not in the sky Da, in the water. What are they, anyway?
EAGLE	Phosphorous.
ISAAC	Phosphorous! I must tell them in school about that on Monday. I bet the teacher don't know about that.
EAGLE	I'm feckin' sure he don't know about it.
ISAAC	The size of that big eel boy! That fella'd nearly turn the boat over wouldn't he? Hah? What would ya do if he turned the boat over, Da?
EAGLE	I don't know.
ISAAC	Can you swim Da?
EAGLE	Yeah of course I can swim.
ISAAC	Can yeh? What's your favorite stroke, the American crawl?
EAGLE	The Japanese flip-flop. Nothin' moves, only your tonsils.
ISAAC	Yeah, 'help, help . . .' A full moon hah? Deadly lookin', ain't it?
EAGLE	Yeah, yeh'd get up in the middle of the night to look at it sure.
ISAAC	(*chuckles*) That's a good one Da. You'd get up in the middle of the night to look at it. You'd hardly see it in the middle of the day would yeh? You should have been a comedian boy!

(*Pause.*)

EAGLE	There she is Isaac. Useless Island. There seems to be a bit of an auld fog comin' down around her.
ISAAC	Yeah, it's queer spooky lookin', ain't it?
EAGLE	Not at all.

(*Slight pause.*)

ISAAC	I don't think me Ma is exactly over the moon about all of this Da, is she?
EAGLE	No, not exactly. Ah she's a bit nervous about it. Yeh see Isaac what she don't understand is that you and me are in our element out here like yeh know. What she don't seem to realise is that this is our what-do-you-call-it . . . What's the word? Domain! But sure I suppose she's listenin' to the rest of them blackguardin' me all the time. I'm not coddin' yeh, for the past twelve months here you'd swear I was committin' some sort of a crime here just comin' out to work. I mean to say I'm only doin' what I always done. Yeh know? I come out here and I cast me nets and I sit and wait. What's wrong with that? Yeh know? No way am I in the wrong, I don't care what anyone says . . . Yeh know sometimes when I'm out here on me own in the middle of the night I'll stand up in the boat like this - sometimes in the middle of the day even - I'll stand up and I look around me. There's the sky and the sea and nothin' else and then I'll let out a sort of a shout out of me. (*He shrieks.*) I'm not coddin' yeh if anyone was watchin' me they'd have me feckin' certified so they would. But do yeh know why I do that? I do it to let this place know that I'm still here, that I'm still around. That's very important yeh know! That way the man learns to respect the place and the place'll respect the man. Me Da taught me that . . . Take a look back at the town.

ISAAC   Oh yeah . . . All the lights! I wonder where our house is? I think I can see my pigeon loft, Da. (EAGLE *smiles at him tenderly*.)

EAGLE   As long as you do your best Isaac, that's all that matters yeh know. You must always do your best. And make the most of what yeh got . . . What's that? A seagull flyin' low be Jaysus!

ISAAC   What do that mean?

EAGLE   Search me. (*He chuckles and sits down again.*)

(*Pause.*)

ISAAC   Do yeh know somethin' Da, I don't think I ever saw you swimmin'. . . Da?

EAGLE   What?

ISAAC   I say I never saw you swimmin'.

EAGLE   Why should I swim when I've got a boat?

(*Pause. Lights down.*)

End of Act One.

ACT TWO

Useless Island. EAGLE *is sitting beside a blazing log fire just in front of the hut. He is drinking a bottle of stout and singing joyfully.* ISAAC *is unpacking one of the cardboard boxes.*

EAGLE (*sings*)
My heart is in Rosa Rio
Under the Argentine skies.
There lives a beautiful lady
With dark and sparkling eyes . . .

(EAGLE *turns to look at his son.*)

What do yeh think of the bed I built for yeh?

ISAAC (*going into the hut*) Grand.

EAGLE Yeah? There's an auld nail above it there in case you're wantin' to hang anythin' up. Do yeh see it?

ISAAC (*in the hut*) Yeah, I just hit me head off of it. (EAGLE *sniggers.* ISAAC *comes back out.*) Hey Da, will you be able to leave me that big flashlight before yeh go?

EAGLE Yeah if yeh like. But sure yeh won't need it anyway Isaac. Before I'm done this fire'll light up the whole island for yeh boy.

ISAAC Oh yeah, me Ma told me to tell yeh that the firelighters are in that auld brown bag there.

EAGLE Firelighters! Do I look like a fella who needs firelighters to light a fire? Now first things first . . . Go get Bridgey Malloy's cake and dump it in the water.

ISAAC What? Now?

EAGLE	Yeah now. I mean to say there's no point in contaminating the atmosphere out here is there Hah? Go ahead. (ISAAC *goes into the hut.*) Did yeh get it?
	(ISAAC *comes out and exits.*)
ISAAC	(*as he goes*) Yeah. I got it.
EAGLE	. . . Are yeh alright?
ISAAC	(*off*) Yeah. Here she goes now.
	(*The sound of the cake splashing into the water is heard off stage.*)
EAGLE	What? Did she sink, yeah?
ISAAC	(*entering*) Yeah, I think so.
EAGLE	Did she what? Like a stone says you . . . Get a cup and pull over to the fire here.
	(ISAAC *gets a mug from one of the boxes and* EAGLE *pours some stout into it. He then proceeds to put a few spoonfuls of sugar into it.*)
	Firelighters! Here, get that into yeh. It'll put a few hairs on your chest.
ISAAC	What? . . . I love the way it all bubbles up when yeh put the sugar into it, do you? Is this part of the tradition too Da, yeah?
EAGLE	Sort of.
ISAAC	What do yeh mean, sort of?
EAGLE	Well my Da did somethin' like this too, the night he brought me out here. Mind you it wasn't exactly like this. He drank about seven large bottles of stout before he went home. Jaysus he was an awful man.

ISAAC	And did he give you a drop in the end of a mug too?
EAGLE	He gave me a whole small bottle to meself so he did. I was half-fluthered drunk before he was gone at all.
ISAAC	What did yeh do after he was gone? Where yeh afraid?
EAGLE	What? No way, Jose. No chance boy! I'll tell yeh now Isaac exactly what I done. I staggered into me hut and I snored like an auld fella all night long.
ISAAC	This'll make me snore Da, won't it?
EAGLE	It'll make yeh fart anyway, whatever about snorin'.
ISAAC	(*singing*) My fart is in Rosa Rio Under the Argentine skies,
EAGLE	(*singing*) There lives a beautiful lady And I bless the day that I die. Aye, yae, aye, yae, yae, yae . . . My heart is in Rosa Rio. (*Pause.*)
ISAAC	Do yeh know somethin' Da, I heard that auld Mosey Brennan saw a mermaid out here one time. Just over there somewhere she was, baskin' in the sun, combin' her hair or somethin'.
EAGLE	That was probably auld Bridgey Malloy washin' her knickers.

ISAAC	What would yeh do though Da if yeh came out one mornin' and found a mermaid tangled up in your net?
EAGLE	What would I do? I'll tell yeh now son I'd throw her back into the sea the same as if she was an auld eel.
ISAAC	Are yeh mad or what, Da. The mermaid I'm talkin' about now is . . . (*He moulds her shape.*) . . . Yeh know, she's really beautiful.
EAGLE	I don't care what she looks like. Half a woman'd be no use to a man like me yeh know . . . Yeh might throw another log on that auld fire there will yeh?
ISAAC	Right.
EAGLE	(*sings*) My heart is in Rosa Rio, Under the Argentine skies . . .
ISAAC	Why couldn't we come out here in the middle of the summer or somethin', Da. I mean to say it's freezin' cauld out here now.
EAGLE	But sure any Jack the Shillin' could come out here in the middle of summer. That's what always amused me about Dribbler and Matty O'Brien and all. They came out here in the middle of the summer. I mean to say where's the point in that. You came out here the same night I did - the tenth of November, St Martin's Eve. Dribbler came out in August or somethin'. . . August be Jaysus!
ISAAC	There's somethin' kind of special about St Martin's Eve, Da ain't there?
EAGLE	Yeah. No self respectin' Wexford fisherman would ever cast a line on St Martin's Eve.
ISAAC	Why not?

EAGLE	I don't know. They're superstitious about it. It's supposed to be unlucky or somethin'. Sure there's a song written about that and everythin'. 'The Fishermen of Wexford', it's called. (*He sings.*)

There is an old tradition sacred held in
    Wexford town
That says upon St Martin's Eve no net shall
    be let down.
No fishermen of Wexford shall upon that
    Holy Day
Set sail or cast a line within the scope of
    Wexford Bay.

The tongue that framed the order or the time
    no one can tell
And no one ever knew it but the people kept
    it well.
And never in man's memory was fisher known
    to leave
The little town of Wexford on the good St
    Martin's Eve.

	That song was written about a disaster that happened here one time. It was on St Martin's Eve and a great big shoal of herring were spotted out beyond the bay. But of course nobody could go out after them because of the day that was in it. All day long the fishermen stood on the shore and watched the gleamin' fish swimmin' past and finally a few fleets decided to disregard the auld tradition and go out after them. Seventy men were lost that day out of this little town boy. That's the last line of the song in fact. 'Seventy fisher's corpses strewed the shores of Wexford Bay.'
ISAAC	Did you ever go out fishin' on St Martin's Eve, Da?
EAGLE	I did. Once and once only. I had a bit of a fire in me belly about somethin' and I refused to

	listen to anyone. I lived to regret it though, I can tell you.
Isaac	Why? What happened?
Eagle	What? Ah I had a bit of bad luck . . .
	(*Slight pause.*)
Isaac	Yeh might tell us about the Dempsey Twins again, Da, will yeh?
Eagle	The Dempsey Twins?
Isaac	Yeah, tell us about them again. I loves hearin' about them boy!
Eagle	Do yeh? . . . The Dempsey Twins used to live around the corner from your granny there, in that little house that what-do-you-call-its are livin' in now.
Isaac	The Byrne's.
Eagle	Yeah. They were more or less the same age as meself and they were absolutely the spittin' image of one another. The only way I was able to tell them apart was that one of them had a slight cast in his eye. And they were inseparable I'm not coddin' yeh. Always together the pair of them. In all the time I knew them I don't think I ever saw one without the other.
Isaac	And supposin' one of them was sick would the two of them stay home from school?
Eagle	Oh yeah. They wouldn't stir without one another sure. They walked the same, talked the same, dressed the same and everythin' . . .
Isaac	Just a minute! Are you tryin' to tell me that if one of them was sick the two of them'd stay home from school?

EAGLE	Are you goin' to let me tell this story or not?
ISAAC	Yeah alright, go ahead.
EAGLE	The two boys were so inseparable that when it came to their turn to go out to the island their Da started kind of wonderin' if maybe it might be alright for them to go out together, seein' how they were never apart before, seein' how they were practically the same fella anyway. But unfortunately their Da was a bit of a pasty-faced sort of a fella - yeh know he was good around the house and all - with the result that nobody really liked him and everybody started sayin' that if the young lads were goin' to go out to the island then it was only right they should go out there alone the same as all the other young lads around here had done. So that's what they done in the end. I'll never forget that night though. The auld shingly beach thronged with people - most of us half hopin' to see the two boys goin' berserk or somethin' But they didn't. They never even flinched boy. The little lad with the cast in his eye just stood beside his mother while the other lad climbed into the boat alongside his Da. One of the other men had to row out to the island because your man was useless with boats . . . None of them cried or nothin' though - although yeh could see that the pair of them were crackin' up inside. To make a long story short anyway in the middle of the night the little lad with the cast in his eye got up out of bed and went down to the water's edge. He could hear his brother cryin' and callin' out his name from the other side and he got so distressed that he kicked off his shoes and tried to swim across to the island just to be near him. But he ran into trouble about half way across and the little lad on the island jumped in and tried to swim to his rescue. Three days later the two dead bodies were fished out of the water.

Auld Mosey Brennan found them tangled up in one of his nets - clingin' together like an auld oyster around a pearl. And I'm goin' to tell yeh one thing but the day they were buried there wasn't a man or woman up around here that didn't hang their heads in shame. Auld Bridgey Malloy said that the poor crators died just because their Da had a pasty face.

(*Silence.*)

ISAAC Well there's twin brothers in my class and they can't stand one another.

EAGLE Listen you don't forget what your Mammy was sayin' to yeh about stayin' away from that fire do yeh hear me?

ISAAC Yeah.

EAGLE And yeh needn't bother your arse goin' down near that water's edge either. There's fifty foot of water there if not more. So stay away from it altogether. Do yeh hear me talkin' to yeh?

ISAAC Yeah . . . What time will you be comin' back to collect me at?

EAGLE The first thing in the mornin' I'll be back out for yeh. It's a pity yeh didn't think of bringin' your big ghetto blaster out with yeh ain't it?

ISAAC Yeah, I forgot all about that.

EAGLE But sure yeh can always read a couple of your comics can't yeh?

ISAAC Yeah. As soon as I finish me porter now I'll read a couple of me comics.

EAGLE Have yeh got everythin' out of the boat now yeh?

Isaac	Yeah I think so. Why, are yeh goin' now?
Eagle	Yeah, I've to go now. Will you be alright?
Isaac	Yeah.
Eagle	Are yeh sure?
Isaac	Yeah.
Eagle	That's good because I've to go and drink a toast to yeh now on the mainland yeh see. (Isaac *chuckles.* Eagle *looks into his son's sad eyes.*) I was the last boy to come out here yeh know! (*Silence.*) I'll see yeh in the mornin' then Isaac, eh?
Isaac	Yeah. Goodbye, Da.
Eagle	Goodbye, son.

(Eagle *leaves. Pause. Lights down. Lights rise. We are in the back room of a pub that is full of people, all drinking and joining in with* Dribbler *as he sings, 'One of the Old Reserves' to a piano accompaniment.*)

They came up from the country,
They came up from the farms.
They came up in their thousands,
When they heard the call to arms.

I wanted to be a soldier boy,
To see what I could gain.
But when I put on the uniform,
It was then that I became

One of the old reserves,
One of the old reserves!

ACT TWO

>Up to the Curragh I was sent,
>That's the place they pay no rent.
>And when the Sergeant saw me,
>He said I did deserve
>Three pints of beer
>Three times a day,
>For being one of the old reserves!

CHORUS
>One of the old reserves,
>One of the old reserves!
>One of the old,
>One of the old,
>One of the old reserves!

>My first night in the cook house,
>My pal he said to me;
>There's something wrong with the cook,
>Because he's giving us eggs for tea.

>Now why he should make this rude remark,
>I really couldn't tell.
>But when I opened up the egg,
>It was then that I got the smell!

>It was one of the old reserves,
>One of the old reserves!

>To eat this egg I did my best,
>It nearly paralysed my chest.
>For a cook to cook this hard boiled egg,
>A shooting he deserved.
>But we let him go
>Because we know
>He was one of the old reserves!

CHORUS
>One of the old reserves,
>One of the old reserves!
>One of the old,
>One of the old,
>One of the old reserves!

>My first night in an army bed,
>Who did I happen to see?
>But crawling on my pillow

Was my good friend mister flea.
He ducked his head in under the sheets,
and whistled up the gang.
They marched in time
and sang in rhyme
And this is the song they sang

We belong to the old reserves,
Belong to the old reserves!
We can sing and we can dance,
We've been to Belgium and to France,
We can bite the knee
and we can surely bite the nerve,
But the sweetest bite we ever got
Was off one of the old reserves!

CHORUS   One of the old reserves,
One of the old reserves!
One of the old,
One of the old,
One of the old reserves!

My first night out in uniform,
I marched across the green.
I met a dainty flapper,
And she looked a sweet sixteen.
She wore a dainty stocking,
She wore a dainty sock,
But when I got up beside her
It was then that I spied the clock!

She was one of the old reserves,
One of the old reserves!
Give us a kiss and I'll love you more,
'Oh no' says I, I've been caught before.
For a man to kiss a clock like that,
A shooting he'd deserve.
So off she flew
Because she knew
I was one of the old reserves!

(*The whole place joins in on the final chorus as* DRIBBLER *does a little nimble dance around the floor.*)

CHORUS	One of the old reserves, One of the old reserves! One of the old, One of the old, One of the old reserves!

(Applause, laughter and cheers from all. General hubbub ensues during the following.)

MOSEY	Well done Dribbler.
ZAK	Oon, Dribbler me boy!
EAGLE	Fair play to yeh Drib . . . !
DRIBBLER	Right lads, a bit of order there now. A bit of hush. Listen to me will yez. Order! I'm wantin' to propose a toast to Eagle and Isaac lads.
MOSEY	Here here Dribbler!
DRIBBLER	Because what Eagle done tonight - bringin' Isaac out to the island and that - well I know it warmed the cockles of my heart anyway whatever about any of the rest of yeh and I'm sure Mosey Brennan there'll agree with me when I say that it's a pity the auld tradition ever died out in the first place.
MOSEY	That's for sure.
DRIBBLER	What it is lads is a gift. A gift from father to a son. And on the eve of St Martin's too, hah!
BROADERS	St Martin's Eve, Dribbler! St Martin's Eve boy!
DRIBBLER	Yeah that as well . . . No but seriously though lads. This is the kind of thing that can't be bought or sold yeh know. Yeh can't bottle it. Yeh can't wrap it up and put it on a shelf somewhere because it's not for sale. I mean to

say I have fond memories meself of the night I spent out on the island. I brought me ferret out with me to keep me company and the little whore ran off huntin' in the bushes the minute I got there and I never saw him no more. A great big bull seal came up on to the island in the middle of the night then and started roarin' and bawlin' in the early hours - frightened the friggin' life out of me so he did. (*Laughter*.) But that was all a long time ago now though lads and things have changed. There was a time when you could look out that window there and you'd see thirty or forty little boats out there - sailin' across the bay after the herring or up the river after the salmon and the fresh water trout, or beyond the bar after the mullet and the mackerel. And in the evenin' they'd all pull into the shelter and you'd hear all the boys laughin' and jokin' and cursing and all. Marian Brennan'd come down with a bowl of soup for Mosey and Bridgey Malloy'd be callin' down to poor auld John-Joe and you'd look up at the sky and yeh'd smell it and yeh'd taste it - the sea and the wind and the rain - and back then there was no reason to believe that it was ever goin' to end but it did. Eagle there is the last of them now and here are we all workin' in the auld factory, fishin' for things we would have slung back once upon a time. We're all only - what's the word Eagle? Shadows of our former selves. That was nice Mosey wasn't it? But of course that's all neither here nor there now. Come on. Raise your glasses. To Eagle and Isaac!

ALL   To Eagle and Isaac.

DRIBBLER   And to Veronica of course for puttin' up with the pair of them.

MOSEY   Well said Dribbler.

(*They drink.* VERONICA *is going round with a tray of food.*)

DRIBBLER (*to* BROADERS) He's one of the best boy, I don't care what anyone says . . .

BROADERS Yeah but what's it all in aid of though Dribbler, that's what I'd like to know. What's it all in aid of?

DRIBBLER Ah in aid of me arse! . . . Put it there Eagle. You're one in a million boy!

EAGLE (*wryly*) I am ain't I?

DRIBBLER Yeah. Yeh are though. I'm goin' to tell yeh one thing now Eagle for nothin' boy . . .

VERONICA Don't strain yourself or anythin' there now Eagle.

EAGLE What?

DRIBBLER Hey Veronica, come here for a minute. (*He draws her towards him.*) Veronica'll vouch for me. She knows I don't bullshit.

VERONICA (*breaking away*) Yeh don't! That's news to me then.

DRIBBLER Hah? Lord Jaysus ain't that awful Eagle. Stymied at every fence boy. Hah? I don't know! No but seriously though Eagle. Straight up. You know me. If I say somethin' I mean it. If I don't mean it I won't say it, do yeh know what I mean?

EAGLE (*eating*) Yeah.

BROADERS Hey Eagle I believe you're joinin' the firm on Monday mornin' is that right? . . . Bright and early hah? You'll find out what hard work is all about then boy . . .

HUMPY	Yeah and yeh needn't think that this little escapade here tonight'll cut any ice either. Last in, first out boy!
DRIBBLER	Yeh may get used to all this Eagle because . . .
BROADERS	And here while we're on the subject, what's all this I hear about your missus being seen drinkin' with your man Collins the teacher last night down in the bar of the Railway Hotel? I hope you're not goin' to let the side down now or anythin' boy.
HUMPY	Yeah while you were out catchin' sardines Eagle she was out gettin' herself edgamacated! (*He laughs.*) I hope yeh don't think that I was being impudent or anythin' there a minute ago Eagle. Just markin' your card for yeh like yeh know. Last into the job first out. Do yeh know what I mean Eagle?
EAGLE	Mmn . . . Jaysus people's atin' habits are terrible strange though lads ain't they? Hah?
HUMPY	How do yeh mean?
EAGLE	Well I mean yeh know how it is like. Some people go to restaurants and ate. Some people go to pubs. Other people love to be surrounded by people when they're atin'. Yeh know they go to dinner dances and what-do-you-call-its?
HUMPY	Reunions?
EAGLE	Yeah. They go to auld reunions and all. Now take me for example. When Eagle is atin' he just likes to be left alone. Do yeh know what I mean?
HUMPY	What?

(BROADERS *chuckles and turns away.* HUMPY *stands there staring into* EAGLE'S *angry eyes.*

Soon he gets the message and turns away sheepishly.)

DRIBBLER (*rising*) Here come on Eagle, I'll give yeh a game of darts.

EAGLE What? Yeah, I'll be out there in a minute.

DRIBBLER What?

BROADERS I'll give yeh a game Dribbler . . . Hey Humpy come on, it's your shout.

HUMPY What?

BROADERS Come on. And bring us me pint there and yeh comin' will yeh.

(*They exit.* EAGLE *sits there brooding.*)

VERONICA Are yeh not eatin' Zak?

ZAK No, I'm not all that hungry to tell yeh the truth.

VERONICA What's wrong with yeh? Sonia?

ZAK It's a wonder she's here at all. Lately when I come in one door she goes out the other. I mean to say I can't even get a chance to what-do-you-call-it like yeh know . . . Ah I don't know. I asked Bridie to try and put in a word for me but . . . She thinks I should just let her go. What do you think?

VERONICA I don't know Zak. Sonia's a bit of a Thumbelina like yeh know.

ZAK How do yeh mean?

VERONICA She knows her way around.

ZAK Does that mean that yeh think I have a chance with her?

VERONICA	Not a lot, no.
	(VERONICA *goes around the room, picking up dirty plates, etc.* BRIDIE *watches her sadly.* EAGLE *exits.*)
BRIDIE	Are yeh alright Mosey?
MOSEY	Yeah. But sure it's grand to have a bit of grub handed to yeh ain't it?
BRIDIE	Mmn . . . Can I give yeh a hand or anythin' Veronica?
VERONICA	What? No, it's alright.
	(VERONICA *exits.*)
BRIDIE	I dare say your auld house feels fairly quiet over there this weather Mosey is it?
MOSEY	Oh stop. It's like a grave sure. Not that meself and the missus ever did a whole lot of talkin' when she was alive anyway. A few auld grunts and growls now and again but nevertheless . . . To tell yeh the truth Bridie, the only noise you're likely to hear over there now is the sound of askin' meself why she ever went and did what she done.
BRIDIE	But sure I suppose the poor crator was distracted Mosey.
MOSEY	Yeah. She must have been alright. Ah I don't think her heart was ever in that auld marriage from the start though yeh know. Her heart was elsewhere I think. I wouldn't mind but I knew that even in the early days only I was too bloody contrary to let her go. Mind you she was a beautiful sight to behold that time - watchin' her risin' up before yeh in the mornin' or seein' her movin' about the house. I was kind of like a man with a beautiful

flower that every one else wanted, knowin' full well in me heart and soul that it was only a matter of time. I used to pray that she'd wilt or wither a little bit just so I'd be allowed to hold on to her a little longer. But she never did. Not to my eyes anyway. And now I keep badgerin' poor little Jimmy O'Keefe the baker to try and tell me everything that he saw that mornin'. I'm sure the man dreads to see me comin' now. But I need to know why she gave herself to the sea like that. I mean to say she always hated the sea. She hated it as much as I loved it yeh know. It's queer ain't it? And here I am now another year and a day later and I'm still none the wiser and everything I thought I'd never be, I am.

BRIDIE I wouldn't say you're none the wiser now Mosey. Yeh found out what love is didn't yeh? What else is there to know?

(VERONICA *returns with a drink for herself. She sits at a table.*)

MOSEY Love? No, I don't think so somehow or other.

BRIDIE What?

(BRIDIE *rises and exits, passing* EAGLE *on his way in. Their eyes meet.* MOSEY *hangs his head sadly.* EAGLE *goes to* VERONICA.)

EAGLE How many people were at the meetin'?

VERONICA I don't know. Eight or nine.

EAGLE And everyone went into the bar afterwards did they?

VERONICA No not everyone. Some of them went straight home and some of them went into the coffee shop.

EAGLE How many went into the bar?

VERONICA	I don't know, I wasn't keepin' track of them.
EAGLE	How many? It was just you and him went into the bar wasn't it?
VERONICA	Yeah as far as I know . . .
EAGLE	What did yeh have?
VERONICA	I had a glass of lager.
EAGLE	How many drinks did yeh have?
VERONICA	Two or three.
EAGLE	Yeah and then what?
VERONICA	How do yeh mean?
EAGLE	Then what did yeh do?
VERONICA	We talked.
EAGLE	What did yeh talk about?
VERONICA	Look Eagle I really don't want to . . .
EAGLE	What did yeh talk about I said.
VERONICA	We talked about things. Different things. Things you wouldn't understand.
EAGLE	Oh things I wouldn't understand hah! All above my head! I had this tossed in my face here tonight yeh know in front of everyone. I mean to say this is exactly the kind of ammunition that they need to cut me off at the knees and here are you handin' it to them on a plate.
VERONICA	If you're not big enough to climb over those crowd of ejits Eagle, then I think you'd better stay out of the water by yourself where you belong.

EAGLE	What's that supposed to mean?
VERONICA	And you're talkin' about makin' a man out of Isaac. Jesus!
EAGLE	No, I'm talkin' about goin' round after school tomorrow and see this fella face to face, that's what I'm talkin' about.
VERONICA	You don't start anythin' here now.
EAGLE	That's what I'm talkin' about.
VERONICA	Eagle you go next or near that man and you'll be kissin' me goodbye boy.
EAGLE	Kissin' yeh goodbye. That'd make a change alright. Kissin' yeh goodbye? Or kissin' yeh hello either for that matter.
VERONICA	What's that supposed to mean? Eagle I'm a woman. And there's things I need to hear before I . . .
EAGLE	Things yeh need to hear! Well there's things I don't need to hear and one of them is that my wife is whorin' around behind my back.
VERONICA	Is that what you think of me? Do you seriously think for one minute that I'd ever do that to you . . .
EAGLE	What do yeh think of that Dribbler? There's things she needs to hear.

(DRIBBLER *is entering with two pints, one for* MOSEY.)

DRIBBLER	What's that?

(VERONICA *throws* EAGLE *a dirty look.* EAGLE *grabs his coat and leaves in a huff.*)

EAGLE	I'm goin' to take a bit of a walk Dribbler. I'll see yeh after.
DRIBBLER	Yeah right Eagle.

(VERONICA *watches* EAGLE *go.* DRIBBLER *takes another sandwich from her tray.*)

VERONICA	What am I goin' to do with that fella Dribbler eh?
DRIBBLER	I don't know. I've no sympathy for yeh. Yeh couldn't wait to get him.
VERONICA	(*chuckles*) That's true . . . But sure you don't care anyway do yeh?
DRIBBLER	No. I mean to say I was the one who saw yeh first anyway.
VERONICA	Yeah?
DRIBBLER	Yeah.
VERONICA	So how come I ended up with him and not with you then?
DRIBBLER	Why does the sun go down? . . . Destiny!

(VERONICA *laughs sadly. She sighs.* BRIDIE *is singing, 'I Let My Hair Down,' out in the other bar.*)

DRIBBLER	Good girl Bridie.

(*Slight pause.*)

VERONICA	Oh I don't know. St Martin's Eve'll be the death of the lot of us yet I think.

(*Lights down. Lights rise on the island.* ISAAC *is sitting over the fire reading a comic. On a nearby hilltop* SONIA *and* BRIAN *are snuggling into one another, looking down on the boy from afar.)*

SONIA Ah, look at the little face on him. He looks lost don't he?

BRIAN Yeah. Cosy but lost. Are yeh wantin' to go down to him?

SONIA No, we can't go down to him. Nobody's supposed to go near him tonight.

BRIAN Well what did we come out here for then?

SONIA Just to make sure that he's alright.

BRIAN Really?

SONIA Mmn . . .

BRIAN That fire looks nice.

SONIA Sssh . . .

BRIAN My hands are cold.

SONIA Are they?

(She looks into his eyes and smiles. They kiss.)

BRIAN Now I think I know what me grandfather saw in this place.

SONIA What, the harbour yeh mean?

BRIAN No. The women!

(She chuckles and bends to kiss him.)

I bet she looked just like you yeh know. Dark and beautiful. And a bit of a mystery! Always a mystery! . . . And when she walked down the street the whole landscape changed. The flowers bowed and swayed, the men stopped workin', the children stopped playin'. Her beautiful curved body. Sure no wonder he wanted to live inside of her!

(They kiss. Slight pause.)

SONIA   I wonder what became of her.

BRIAN   I wonder what became of the diary.

SONIA   She probably went back to her husband. And spent the rest of her life in the arms of a man she didn't really love . . . I could never do that. When I give my love away it'll be with absolute certainty. Only he'll never know.

BRIAN   He'll never know that you love him?

SONIA   He'll never know how much I love him. And he'll never know the lengths I'll go to to make him want me.

(BRIAN *chuckles softly at her wisdom. He strokes her hair.*)

BRIAN   I don't think my grandda ever got over her yeh know, not according to that auld diary anyway. And he never really trusted anyone again after that either. He always was so full of hatred that he couldn't even bring himself to acknowledge his own grandchildren. He drove his whole family away sure. The only time I've ever seen a pair of eyes so full of hatred was the other day when I was givin' Broaders a bollockin' for being late. Smoulderin' they were nearly! . . . I feel fairly at home here now though yeh know. I mean I seem to have spent my whole life wanderin' aimlessly from one place to another - colleges and cafes, cathedral bells everywhere. Stoppin' at a stall to buy a book I'll never read, takin' it back to my attic or my little basement flat, always makin' sure to move on of course before anyone had the chance to root me down. I was goin' to be a high flier yeh see - although in my heart and soul I knew I'd probably settle for some easy option in the end. That's why I'm glad I had the chance to come back and take over the place. I mean I know I'm only a blow in and all, but . . . Well I'm glad I came back anyway . . . I found these pictures of Menapia Mansion in an auld cardboard box yeh know. Little sort of postcards that were printed of it. It looked like a lovely place alright - the house, the gardens, even the factory had a certain flair about it.

(*He shakes his head and sighs.*)

SONIA But sure maybe you'll put it all back together again?

BRIAN Mmn, that'd be somethin' alright wouldn't it? Put it all back together again and then when no one was lookin' just slip quietly away.

SONIA I love it when you're serious . . . The little wrinkles around your eyes and all. And in the office when yeh put on your glasses. Sometimes I see yeh through the window. Yeh always look so intelligent or somethin'.

BRIAN I am intelligent.

SONIA Yeah but yeh don't always look it.

BRIAN Thanks very much

(*They cuddle into each other.*)

SONIA Bridie says that I should try and hang on to you yeh know - that you'd make a good catch.

BRIAN Is that what you're lookin' for - a good catch?

SONIA Well I'm hardly lookin' for a bad one now am I?

(BRIAN *laughs and lays his head in her lap.*)

BRIAN
Me poor grandda walked on a snare I think . . . And here am I followin' in his footsteps.

SONIA
Yeah, you'd want to be careful Brian. The place is probably mined yeh know.

(*They kiss. Lights down. Lights rise. The graveyard.* BROADERS, ZAK *and* HUMPY *enter, drinking from flagons of cider.*)

HUMPY
Do yeh know what gets on my nerves Broaders? Bridie singin' that auld song all the time. The same auld song all the time she sings boy don't she? That gets on my nerves boy! And Dribbler is as bad. (*He sings scoffingly.*) 'One of the auld reserves, one of the auld reserves . . .' It'd put years on yeh wouldn't it? Hah?

ZAK
Shut up Humpy will yeh, they're right behind us yeh know.

HUMPY
I'm worried about them now Zak!

BROADERS
Bullshit! . . . that's what I hate.

HUMPY
What?

BROADERS
Bullshit! . . . I look around me and all I see is bullshit. Grown men walkin' around with their tails between their legs be Jaysus. I see Dribbler - bullshittin'. And I see Eagle.

HUMPY
Bullshittin'!

BROADERS
I see Mosey.

HUMPY
Bullshittin'!

BROADERS
And Bridie!

HUMPY
Bullshittin'!

BROADERS   And I see me.

HUMPY   Bullshittin'!

(BROADERS *throws him a dirty look.*)

BROADERS   I see me inventin' a new language. A new way of lookin' at things.

HUMPY   How do yeh mean?

BROADERS   The mark of the crab!

HUMPY   Yes.

BROADERS   (*holding his drink aloft*) To the mark of the crab!

HUMPY   Gullagullagoo . . . yip, yip, yip . . .

BROADERS   (*inhaling*) I need to do somethin', take somebody down a peg or two!

HUMPY   Yes!

(HUMPY *grins with excitement.* DRIBBLER *and* BRIDIE *enter. She goes to the grave.*)

DRIBBLER   That was a right auld session though all the same lads wasn't it? Hah?

HUMPY   Bullshit Dribbler. A load of bullshit boy!

DRIBBLER   What? Well I enjoyed it anyway.

ZAK   And fuck the begrudgers Dribbler, ain't that right?

DRIBBLER   Exactly!

BROADERS   I'm goin' to tell yeh one thing Dribbler but the way you were goin' on tonight about

	Eagle anyone'd think he was after walkin' on the water or somethin'.
DRIBBLER	I never said the man walked on the water at all.
BROADERS	I mean to say that's alright Dribbler but . . . livin' in the past is all very well but I mean to say there's much more interestin' stories around than the ones you fellas keep tellin' us all the time yeh know. Stories of unborn bastards for instance and young women growin' old before their time. Night time stories Dribbler like yeh know. Night time stories boy!
HUMPY	Well if it's night time stories you're wantin' Broaders, I'll give yeh a right one now. (*He takes out the diary.*) If I can find it . . . Hey Dribbler, he said he wanted to live inside of her!
DRIBBLER	Who?
HUMPY	Taylor's grandda. Do yeh know what he died of Dribbler? Hornitus! Accordin' to this anyway.
DRIBBLER	What is that loola on about eh?
BROADERS	I'm goin' to do somethin' . . . Come on, let's do something.
HUMPY	What? . . . Where are yeh goin' Broaders.
BROADERS	Let's do somethin'.
HUMPY	Hah? Yes! Come on Zak, we're goin' to do somethin'. Gullagullagoo . . . Hey Dribbler, a load of bullshit boy!

(*The three boys exit. Pause.* DRIBBLER *turns to find* BRIDIE *standing over the little overgrown grave.*)

DRIBBLER	What's up Bridie? Are yeh alright?
BRIDIE	Yeah.
DRIBBLER	What? . . . What's wrong?
BRIDIE	This is my baby's grave Dribbler.
DRIBBLER	Yeah I know.
BRIDIE	This is the first time you've ever come up here with me and this is my baby's grave. I know yeh think yeh love me and all. Yeh act as if yeh love me and yeh look as if yeh love me and yet this is the first time yeh ever visited the grave with me. Part of me is buried here too yeh know. It shapes nearly everythin' I do and say, everythin' I am really. And you've never been here before have yeh? My baby's grave! He must have been the quietest boy that ever was born. He came into the world and went back out of it again without makin' a sound. We buried him without makin' a sound and I mourned him without a sound too - pacin' up and down me bedroom floor. Tiptoein' to work in the mornin's, everythin' kind of muffled. Days, weeks, months, years - everything muffled . . . And now it's the tenth of November again - St Martin's Eve - and this is my baby's grave. If he had lived he would have been thirteen today - old enough to go out to the island . . . And I'll tell yeh somethin' else for nothin' Dribbler, it breaks my heart to think that his Daddy has never even come here to say a few prayers for him or to put a few flowers on his grave. Yes, this is my baby's grave and not a day goes by that I don't think of him and mourn for him. Not a day boy!
DRIBBLER	Sure I know that Bridie. Anyone who ever listened to yeh singin'd know that . . . I'm goin' to tell yeh one thing but I'm comin' up

here tomorrow to clean up that auld grave.
And I'm going' to paint that auld cross too, I
don't mind tellin' yeh. We should get a
proper headstone for here anyway. Sure who
knows, maybe we'll all be lyin' in there
beside him one of these days hah?

(BRIDIE *smiles through her tears. She blesses
herself and mouths a silent prayer. Pause.
Lights down. Lights rise on the island.* ISAAC
*is sitting in front of his hut. He rises,
stretches himself and yawns. The wind rustles.
He picks up his flashlight and shines it into
the bushes, singing to hide his fear.*)

ISAAC (*sings*)
There is an old tradition
Sacred held in Wexford Town
That says upon St Martin's Eve
No net shall be let down

(*He gathers his things together and goes into
the hut for the night.*)

No fishermen of Wexford
Shall upon that holy day
Set sail or cast a line . . .

(*Lights down. Lights rise on the graveyard
where* EAGLE *is standing over the baby's
grave. He has a bunch of wildflowers which
he places on the grave. He blesses himself.
Pause.* VERONICA *enters. Pause. He goes to
her and takes her in this arms, falling to his
knees to bury his head into her body. She hugs
him tearfully to her. Lights down. Lights rise.
Useless Island. Night time.* BROADERS *is
kicking the fire alive.* ZAK *is sitting beside the
hut, drinking.* HUMPY *is on the roof of the hut,
howling like a wolf.* ISAAC *comes out to shine
his flashlight up into* HUMPY'S *face.*)

HUMPY The face of him!

ISAAC	What are you all doin' out here? No one's supposed to come out here tonight yeh know.
BROADERS	That's the thanks we get now lads.
ISAAC	What?
ZAK	It's alright Isaac, stop worryin' will yeh.
ISAAC	Stop worryin' he says!
BROADERS	So this is the famous hut then is it? We never saw one of these before yeh know. We were all deprived.
HUMPY	Yeah, we were all deprived. (*He pretends to weep.*) What kind of sandwiches have yeh got boy?
	(HUMPY *jumps down and takes* ISAAC's *lunch box.*)
ISAAC	Hey Humpy, give them back to me.
HUMPY	(*eating a sandwich*) What?
ISAAC	Cut it out Humpy, they've to last me all night yeh know. I'm goin' to tell me Da on you in the mornin' boy.
HUMPY	Go ahead and tell him, I don't care. I'm only feedin' the poor auld seagulls anyway. Here chuck. Here chuck, chuck, chuck . . .
BROADERS	So tell us how does it feel to be a man boy? Do yeh feel it all seepin' through yeh now yeah? Hah? Do yeh? Yeah? Hah? (*He crowds* ISAAC.)
ISAAC	Go away from me Broaders will yeh.
BROADERS	Hah?
HUMPY	Are these all the comics yeh have?

ZAK	Bad news for yeh Isaac, it looks like I'm not goin' to be your uncle after all.
HUMPY	Yeah so give him back all the money he gave yeh . . .
BROADERS	Hey boy, I hope you don't think that this is going to make you a big shot around here now or anythin'. Just because you're the only one to come out here and all.
ZAK	But sure he is the only one. Ain't yeh, Isaac?
ISAAC	I don't know. I suppose I am. But sure me Da was the last boy to come out here yeh know - before me I mean. (BROADERS *scoffs*.) What's so funny Broaders, he's better than you anyway.
BROADERS	Oh yeah? In what way like?
ISAAC	Every way.
BROADERS	In what way is he better than me though?
ISAAC	Every way I said . . .
BROADERS	What?
ISAAC	He goes his own way and that.
BROADERS	He goes his own way?
ISAAC	Yeah.
BROADERS	What do yeh mean he goes his own way like?
ISAAC	He goes his own way that's all. He don't have to answer to no one nor nothin'.
BROADERS	Why who do I have to answer to?
ISAAC	Yeh have to answer to your boss - the fella that owns the factory or whatever yeh want to call him.

BROADERS	But sure your Da'll have to start answerin' to him next week.
ISAAC	How do yeh mean?
BROADERS	Your Da is turnin' into work in the factory on Monday mornin' boy. Bright and early!
ISAAC	Who told you that? He never said nothin' to me about that then.
BROADERS	Yeah well he wouldn't would he? That's what this is all in aid of sure. You've been brought and sold down the river boy so yeh have.
ISAAC	I don't believe you.
BROADERS	Suit yourself.

(ISAAC *looks from* BROADERS *to* ZAK *to* HUMPY.)

ISAAC	Go away, yeh liar Broaders!
BROADERS	(*viciously grabbing* ISAAC *by the wrists*) Now you listen to me boy, Broaders may be a whole lot of things but one thing he never is is a liar and don't you ever forget that.

(BROADERS *releases* ISAAC *and seeing the medal he rips it from around his neck, looks at it and throws it to the ground. Then he turns away and goes to the fire.*)

ZAK	(*singing*) There is an old tradition Sacred held in Wexford Town That says upon St Martin's Eve No net shall be let down . . .

(ISAAC *feels his sore wrists and bends to pick up the medal.*)

Yeh missed a right session in the pub tonight Isaac.

ISAAC	Yeah? Why was there a bit of a singsong there and all yeah?
ZAK	Yeah there was a right singsong there boy. We all drank a toast to you and all sure.
ISAAC	Who was there?
ZAK	Everyone. Mosey and Dribbler and all. A right session it was, boy.
ISAAC	Did Dribbler sing, 'One Of The Old Reserves'?
ZAK	Yeah.
ISAAC	And did he do all the actions to it and all?
ZAK	The whole works boy. And your Da sang, 'The Fishermen of Wexford.'
ISAAC	Did he? That's a deadly song ain't it?
ZAK	Deadly!
HUMPY	(*chuckling at the comic*) Look at the little skinny head on your man, Isaac.
ISAAC	Who? Show us. Oh yeah, I loves him. There's a lad in my class and he has a head just like that yeh know.
HUMPY	Your man has a neck like a corkscrew hasn't he?
ZAK	What are yeh doin' Broaders, countin' the stars of what?
BROADERS	What?
ZAK	Can yeh see what it's all in aid of out there yeah?
HUMPY	(*pointing to the comic*) What do that mean?

ISAAC	Von't. So yeh von't talk hah?
HUMPY	Von't?
ISAAC	He's a German Humpy. A Nazi! So yeh von't talk hah?
HUMPY	(*bewildered*) Hah? How can the man talk and he gagged?
ISAAC	Exactly!

(ZAK *lilts 'The Fishermen of Wexford.'*)

BROADERS	Me granny used to bring me out here every year for a day when I was a young fella yeh know. 'We're goin' out to the island tomorrow,' she'd say out of the blue as if she had just got an invisible signal or somethin'. And I'd be sent off to the shop for the lemonade and biscuits while she made the sandwiches. Me grandda'd drop us off here on his way to work and meself and me granny'd go tiptoein' around this auld island like a couple of intruders . . . She used to stand on top of that little hill over there. She'd close her eyes and let the wind blow through her hair. She'd pick up a handful of sand and watch it tricklin' through her fingers. She'd hold a queer lookin' shell against her ear and listen to the sea. Later on I'd go prowlin' around the island and she'd sit over there somewhere readin' a book and every time I'd sneak up behind her I'd find her starin' into space, the book lyin' open in her lap, miles away! . . . And I'd crouch down behind an auld wall and call out to her. Thumbelina! Thumbelina! . . . It was out here one day that she made me promise her that when I was old enough I'd sprout a pair of wings and fly away. She showed me a paintin' of a white winged horse and I used to picture meself flyin' off on it - up over the town, up over the

houses, away over the island. And I'd hear her callin' out to me to never come back. 'You don't belong here,' she said. 'Go away and never come back' . . . Never come back! Of course I didn't know then that she was goin' to go away without me. I always thought she'd be here to see me go.

(*Silence.*)

ZAK (*reciting*)
There is an old tradition sacred in Wexford town
That says upon St Martin's Eve no net shall be let down.
No fisherman of Wexford shall upon that holy day
Set sail or cast a line within' the scope of Wexford Bay.

(*He begins to beat out a rhythm on an old wooden box. After a while* HUMPY *becomes infected and he too begins to beat an old tin can. There is something savage about the sound.*)

The tongue that framed the order or the time no man can tell
And no one ever knew it but the people kept it well
For never in man's memory was fisher known to leave
The little town of Wexford on the good St Martin's Eve.

(*The rhythm climbs towards a savage crescendo.*)

Alas! Alas for Wexford! once upon that holy day
Came a wondrous shoal of herring to the waters of the bay
The fishers and their families stood out upon the beach

ACT TWO

  And all day watched with wistful eyes the
   wealth they might reach.

  Such shoal was never seen before and keen
   regret went round
  Alas! Alas for Wexford! Hark! What is that
   grating sound?
  The boat's keel on the shingle, Mothers!
   Wives ye well may grieve
  The fishermen of Wexford mean to sail on
   Martin's Eve.

(*The drumming is at feverish pitch now.* SONIA *enters with* BRIAN *trailing slightly behind her.*)

  'Oh stay ye,' cried the women wild.
  'Stay!' cried the men white-haired
  And dare ye not to do the thing
  Your fathers never . . .

(*The song trails off at the sight of* SONIA *and* BRIAN *approaching.* HUMPY *does not see them and continues to drum.*)

BROADERS Well what do yeh know Isaac, Aunty Sonia and Uncle Whatshisname have come to pay a call.

ISAAC What? Ah for God's sake, what is this a feckin' reunion or somethin'?

HUMPY Hey Isaac, I thought no one was supposed to come out here tonight.

ISAAC What are youse wantin'?

SONIA Now Isaac don't get excited. Calm down. What are you doin' out here Zak?

ZAK What am I doin' out here! (*He shakes his head in disgust.*)

BROADERS	(*sticking his knife in the fire*) It's alright Sonia. We only came out to make sure that the young fella was alright like yeh know. Yeh see sometimes these courtin' couples come out here to screw in the bushes and that, and we just thought that Isaac might get a bit of a fright when he'd hear them gruntin' and groanin' like yeh know.
	(HUMPY *titters*.)
BRIAN	What's goin' on?
BROADERS	And the dead arose and appeared to many.
BRIAN	What?
BROADERS	I was just sayin' here Mister New Boss Man that we only came out to try and bring it home to Isaac that this heap of shite that he's been sleepin' in tonight is no longer what-do-you-call-it around here any more . . . What's the word Zak? Valid! That's it. It's out of date. Old hat! Yeah. This is the baby now if you're wantin' to keep abreast of things around here. The mark of the crab!
HUMPY	Yes!
BROADERS	So we decided to come out and initiate Isaac into the gang. Ain't that right Isaac?
ISAAC	No way Broaders! I'm not lettin you next or near my arm, boy.
BROADERS	What?
SONIA	I think we're goin' to have to take Isaac back into town with us.
BRIAN	Alright.
ISAAC	Into town! I can't go back into town until the mornin'.

SONIA   Look Isaac, I'll explain it all to your Daddy when we get home.

ISAAC   Ah Sonia . . .

BROADERS   It's reddenin' up Isaac.

ISAAC   What?

BROADERS   It's reddenin' up.

ISAAC   Will you shut up Broaders and leave me alone.

BROADERS   (*taking the red hot knife out of the fire*) Oh yes, I think so.

BRIAN   Cut it out Broaders will yeh, you're frightenin' the young fella.

BROADERS   (*putting the knife back into the fire again*) What?

BRIAN   Cut it out I said.

BROADERS   (*rising*) You must think that you're still in the factory or somethin' do yeh? Givin' orders there!

BRIAN   Get your things together Isaac and come on.

ISAAC   Tch . . . (*He begins to gather up his belongings.*)

BROADERS   (*shoving* BRIAN *around, trying to humiliate him*) Yes, givin' orders there if yeh don't mind. Givin' orders. Who do you think yeh are, eh boy? Hah? Givin' orders. Hah? I mean to say you're not in the factory now or anythin' yeh know. Givin' orders.

BRIAN   Grow up Broaders, will yeh.

BROADERS	A hard case with a soft suitcase there, givin' orders.
SONIA	Leave him alone Broaders.
BROADERS	Mouth almighty, givin' orders.
	(HUMPY *titters*.)
ISAAC	I'm goin' to tell me Da on you in the mornin' Broaders.
BRIAN	Come on Isaac will yeh.
ISAAC	Yeah, just a minute.
SONIA	Hurry up Isaac.
BROADERS	You must think that yeh own the place up around here now or somethin' do yeh? Hah?
BRIAN	No I don't think I own the place at all.
BROADERS	What?
	(BRIAN *looks to see* BROADERS *staring into his eyes. Silence.* BROADERS *sniggers and begins to walk away, turning quickly to punch* BRIAN *in the stomach and hitting him with a rabbit punch in the back of the neck as he goes down.* HUMPY *immediately pounces on him, yelping as he proceeds to kick* BRIAN *viciously in the side and sitting on his back and forcing his face into the dirt and so on.* SONIA *runs between them but she is thrown to the ground.* ZAK *tries to separate them too.*)
ZAK	That's enough Broaders, take it easy will yeh.
SONIA	Broaders! Come up off of him Humpy.
BROADERS	Yes, givin' orders there if yeh don't mind.
ISAAC	Leave him alone Broaders. Leave him alone I said.

ACT TWO

HUMPY   I'll tell yeh what we'll do Broaders we'll tie him up with his own tie. And then we'll give him the mark of the crab, seein' how he has a burnin' desire to be one of us. On the forehead, so everyone can see it.

(HUMPY *ties* BRIAN's *hands behind his back with the tie that he has ripped from around* BRIAN's *neck.*)

ISAAC   (*calling out*) Da! Da . . . Help Da . . . !

SONIA   You do Broaders and I swear . . .

BRIAN   Let me up Humpy. Come up off of me I said.

HUMPY   Do yeh hear him Broaders. Givin' orders again. You're in no position to give anybody any orders boy. (*He takes out the diary.*) First I'm goin' to read you a little night time story. Do you recognise this? (*He sniggers.*) Right. 'She uttered the immortal words to me again last night. 'I love you too,' I said, as the night came down around us . . .' But unfortunately bad news for him on the very next page. 'She never showed up last night. Something is wrong I'm afraid.' That was July fourth. 'July the fifth. Still no sign of her. Where can she be. It's over I think. I've lost her. And I'm lost without her. Oh yes my Thumbelina sure knows her way around!' . . . What do yeh make of that? Your grandda was sufferin' from a severe case of . . .

(BROADERS *face darkens. He leaves the blade in the fire and comes across to snatch the diary from* HUMPY's *hand. He reads it and with a furious roar throws it out to sea.*)

HUMPY   Hey Broaders, what are yeh doin' boy.

BROADERS   (*pulling back* BRIAN's *head*) You leave things where they fall in future Mister. Hold his head back there Humpy.

HUMPY	Yes!
SONIA	Zak, you'd better stop them. Do yeh hear me Zak.
ZAK	That's enough Broaders, the game's over.
BROADERS	(*at the fire*) Hah?
ZAK	The game's over I said. Come up off of him Humpy. (ZAK *grabs* HUMPY *by the hair and throws him to the ground.*) Come up off of him I said.
BROADERS	Is there somethin' wrong with you Zak?
ZAK	No, there's nothin' wrong with me at all. You're the one who'd want to take a good look in the mirror at himself boy, not me.

(ZAK *bends to untie* BRIAN'S *hands.*)

BROADERS	What are yeh doin' Zak?
ZAK	I'm lettin' him go. Isaac get your things and bring them down to the boat.
BROADERS	Leave him.
ZAK	What?
BROADERS	Leave him I said. I'm goin' to brand that bastard. Hold his head back Humpy.
HUMPY	What?
BROADERS	Hold his head.
ZAK	(*rising*) Don't start now Broaders.
BROADERS	Why?
ZAK	Because the game's over that's why.

BROADERS	Turnin' against us now are we?
ZAK	Yeah, if helpin' the man up and down to the boat is turnin' against yeh then yeah I'm turnin' against yeh. Alright? Are yeh satisfied now?
BROADERS	I'm goin' to tell yeh one thing Zak but you're some turncoat alright boy.
ZAK	(*bending to untie* BRIAN's *hands*) Yeah, sure.
	(*Suddenly* BROADERS *in a fit of rage raises the knife and brings it down into* ZAK's *arm.* ZAK *cries out in pain and falls to the ground.*)
ISAAC	(*running to the hilltop*) Da! Da! Help Da . . . Help!
	(BROADERS *hovers over* ZAK *who instinctively crawls away from the shuffling feet about him.*)
BROADERS	That's it Zak, you crawl on your belly boy. Slither like an auld eel there, that's all you were ever any good for anyway. Well not Broaders. I'll crawl for no one nor nothin'! Never! And I'll answer to no one either. Because if you think now Zak that I'm goin' to stand around listenin' to some auld fella yearnin' for the past then you've another thing comin' to yeh boy. The here and now is what matters to me mate. Now! Right now! Today! So while you're sittin' here waitin' for judgment day to come I'm goin' to be out there take, take takin' all the time. Because this is the bottom of the barrel we're all slidin' around in now Zak yeh know. The greedy bastards took it all and left us nothin'. Except this of course. (*The hut.*) I forgot all about this - our inheritance! Well do yeh want to know what I think about this Zak? Here's what I think about it.

(*He runs to the fire and takes out a few burning branches and throws them into the hut. Then he rips the sides of the hut apart, kicking them etc, as the smoke begins to billow out of the hut.*)

That's what I think of that . . . Queer ignorant ain't I? A real savage boy! But yeh see the problem is Zak I don't believe in fairy tales any more like yeh know! (*He shrugs.*)

ISAAC (*from the hilltop*) Da! Da! Help Da! Help! . . .

(*Pause.* BROADERS *turns and gazes up at the heavens, his eyes brimming with tears.*)

BROADERS 'Go away and never come back,' she said . . . Never come back!

ISAAC Help Da, Help! . . .

BROADERS (*looking into* BRIAN'S *frightened eyes*) What are you lookin' at? What's the matter, are yeh wantin' to make sure that you'll know me the next time we meet or somethin' is that it? Well here - just so you'll know me. (BROADERS *takes the hot knife and holds it to* BRIAN'S *head. He looks deep into* BRIAN'S *eyes and seems to see himself there. Then suddenly he takes the red hot blade and holds it to his own forehead. He roars out in pain and slowly sinks to his knees, burying his head in the dirt to stifle his cries.* SONIA *runs to free* BRIAN'S *hands.* HUMPY *stands there stunned.* ISAAC *runs back to* SONIA'S *arms.* MOSEY *arrives.*)

MOSEY What's goin' on here? . . . What have yeh done boy?

(*Slowly* BROADERS *raises his head to reveal the mark of the crab burnt into his forehead. He rises from his knees, backs away in shame and dropping the knife turns to flee. Pause. Lights down. Lights rise.* DRIBBLER *is in the little graveyard, clipping the grass on the grave etc. The cross has been painted white.* ISAAC *arrives with a bunch of flowers.*)

ISAAC Here y'are Dribbler, me Mammy sent these up to yeh.

DRIBBLER Oh right, thanks Isaac. Put them there in that auld urn will yeh . . . An eventful night last night by all accounts?

ISAAC Yeah, it surely was. Them fellas are all mad Dribbler! I wouldn't mind but nobody was supposed to come next or near me last night yeh know.

DRIBBLER Yeah well I wouldn't worry too much about that if I was you Isaac. From what I was told I think yeh came through it all with flyin' colours boy. Yes, flying' colours!

ISAAC Did yeh hear what Broaders did?

DRIBBLER Yeah.

ISAAC Set fire to me hut and everything he did. I'm goin' to tell yeh one thing Dribbler but he was queer lucky that me Da didn't catch him this mornin' because he'd've kilt him. Mosey thinks he's after headin' for London or somewhere. He burnt the mark of the crab into his forehead yeh know.

DRIBBLER So I heard. He'd be a nice sight to behold now down around Camden Town or somewhere wouldn't he? Hah?

ISAAC Me Da gave Humpy O'Brien the greatest kick in the arse he ever got boy. And the blood was pumpin' out of the other fella.

DRIBBLER Who's that?

ISAAC	Zak. Sonia went off in the ambulance with him yeh know.
DRIBBLER	Aye?
ISAAC	That's lookin' alright now Dribbler ain't it? (*The grave.*)
DRIBBLER	Not bad.
ISAAC	Did yeh know me Da is turnin' in the factory on Monday?
DRIBBLER	Yeah, I know.
ISAAC	You'll all be workin' there then Dribbler.
DRIBBLER	Yeah . . . By the time you're old enough to manage the factory we'll have the place hoppin' for yeh so we will.
ISAAC	Me workin' there! You must be jokin' Dribbler. No way boy!
DRIBBLER	Why, what are yeh goin' to do instead?
ISAAC	I don't know. I'm not goin' to work there anyway, that's for sure. I'll probably go out fishin' Dribbler, like me Da used to do. All the fish'll be after comin' back by then yeh see and I'll be the only one who knows where to find them. And I'll only take what I need to live on, just the bare amount . . . I'd say I'd make a good fisherman though Dribbler would you? Hah?
DRIBBLER	Yeah.
ISAAC	I will boy!

(ISAAC *whistles, 'The Fishermen of Wexford,' as he watches* DRIBBLER *working. The lights fade.*)

I Let My Hair Down

Billy Roche

One Of the Old Reserves

Billy Roche